MR PUNCH'S
HISTORY OF THE
GREAT WAR

Peace—The Sower

MR PUNCH'S
HISTORY OF THE
GREAT WAR

NONSUCH

To the Reader

For whatsoever worth or wit appears
In this mixed record of five hectic years,
This tale of heroes, heroines—and others—
Thank first "O. S." and then his band of brothers
Who took their cue, with pencil and with pen,
From the gay courage of our fighting men.
Theirs be the praise, not his, who here supplies
Merely the editorial hooks and eyes
And, rich by proxy, prodigally spends
The largess of his colleagues and his friends.

C. L. G.

First published 1920
Copyright © in this edition Nonsuch Publishing Limited, 2007

Nonsuch Publishing Limited
The Mill, Brimscombe Port, Stroud, Gloucestershire, GL5 2QG
www.nonsuch-publishing.com

Nonsuch Publishing is an imprint of NPI Media Group Limited

British Library Cataloguing in Publication Data.
A catalogue record for this book is available from the British Library.

ISBN 978 1 84588 368 3

Typesetting and origination by Nonsuch Publishing Limited
Printed in Great Britain by Oaklands Book Services Limited

Contents

Introduction to the Modern Edition

During the First World War a new weapon emerged in the struggle for victory, one that had never before been tactically employed during wartime. This weapon was propaganda, and, while fighting raged between the soldiers at the front lines, a fierce propaganda battle had commenced far away from the horrors of the trenches between the Central powers and the Allies, a battle that was to play a small but important role in the eventual Allied victory.

Following the outbreak of hostilities in August 1914, it soon became clear that public opinion was going to be an important factor in the success of the war. Maintaining high levels of support would be paramount to the continuing recruitment of the troops that were required for the battlefields. When, during the first weeks of the conflict, the British government discovered that Germany had established a Propaganda Agency, it was news that compelled them to address their own efforts in this area with some urgency. Consequently, the government recognised that a formal body which could both create propaganda and control the flow of information would be invaluable, and, pressed by the need to combat the effects of the German material that was appearing abroad, and to maintain the all-important morale on the home front, the British War Propaganda Bureau was created. David Lloyd George, then Chancellor of the Exchequer, was charged with the task of setting up this organisation, and he appointed Charles Masterman as its head. Wellington House became the bureau's headquarters, and, hidden behind the offices of the National Insurance Department, its very existence was kept a highly guarded secret, even from the majority of British MPs.

The early aims of the bureau were to discuss the best ways of controlling information and promoting Britain's interests during the war. Many ideas were formulated to achieve these objectives. A first step was initiated by Masterman. He called a group of twenty-five leading British authors to a secret meeting in which they could discuss their thoughts and ideas, and, most importantly, be recruited to write pamphlets and books that would promote the government's views on the progress of the war. Many of them complied, including Arthur Conan Doyle, Rudyard Kipling, Arnold Bennett and G.K. Chesterton, and publishers such as Hodder & Stoughton and Oxford University Press agreed to print the material. Pamphlets which had a significant effect on encouraging recruitment were produced, notable examples including Conan Doyle's *To Arms!* and *Over There: War Scenes on the Western Front*, written by Bennett following a visit to the front, in which he disguised his horror at what he had actually witnessed there. Such material achieved a significant success in inciting young men to enlist for the army in droves, by utilising the literary skills of these men to portray the idealised, patriotic image of war that the government wished to promote. Despite this early success, a fear always remained that the British public would eventually become war-weary and that their support would be lost, particularly as the fighting began to drag on far longer than had been initially predicted. New tactics that could boost morale were constantly being sought, and when Lloyd George became prime minister in 1916 the war propaganda effort that had begun at Wellington House was now re-structured and streamlined, with a new Department of Information replacing the bureau. It was later absorbed by a larger Ministry of Information in 1918, headed by Lord Beaverbrook, the owner of the *Daily Express*, and was an organisation which reflected the culmination of the propaganda effort that had been steadily developed by the British government since the onset of the war.

The specific needs of propaganda aimed at the home front were addressed by the National War Aims Committee. This was set up in 1917, and worked closely with the Department of Information to initiate new measures that focused on propaganda in Britain. It is undisputed that the continuing wartime consensus in Britain was partly due to the effect that propaganda had on people's beliefs about the progress of, and justifications for, the war. One of the most valuable outcomes of government propaganda was the unifying effect it could have on the British nation. It aimed to strengthen the spirits of the people by giving them a common purpose, as well as encouraging them to mobilise as a workforce to boost their country's economic stability. This was particularly important when it became clear that the war would not be the short-lived conflict people had expected, and the zeal for voluntary enlistment began to decline. As a response to this, magazines such as *Punch* took a pro-conscription stance, hoping to encourage popular approval for the idea of coerced involvement in the war. It did this by portraying the typical English soldier, epitomised by the character of 'Tommy,' as morally superior to those of the enemy. It was his strength of character and sheer determination that would award him victory over even the most formidable of German soldiers, rather than his military prowess. In this way the character purported to represent the national identity of the British people, by implying that accepting one's duty to fight was really an opportunity to reject past weakness, and embrace the heroic virtues innate in every British subject. Rejection of these ideas would, it was hoped, make people feel they were denying their national duty. *Punch* thus celebrated not only the concept of military victory in the war, but also the ideological conquest of the nation's spirit and courage over the 'alien' armies of the enemy, and it was propaganda material such as this that glorified war and subsequently maintained support for it at a time when it had begun to weaken.

The idea of the 'alien' enemy was certainly a powerful tool. It was mainly perpetuated by keeping feelings of outrage against them at their highest pitch, through 'atrocity' propaganda which dehumanised the German people and justified the need to 'destroy' or 'eliminate' the evil they represented. Newspaper reports used shock-tactic headlines, designed to stir up the emotions of their readers. Infamous examples include 'Germans crucify Canadian Officer', and 'Belgian child's hands cut off by Germans'. Whether these were accurate or not mattered little, as long as they had the desired effect of strengthening the current of hatred against the enemy. It was also seen as imperative to quell any questions about the justifications for the war which were beginning to arise, by restricting information that told of the realities of conditions for the troops, and of the massive loss of life that was resulting from the fighting. Newspapers therefore reported casualty figures that were acceptable to the government, but far from accurate. The truth of what was happening at the front was further guarded by only two sanctioned photographers being permitted to take pictures; anyone else would face the penalty of a firing squad. Artists were also commissioned to produce drawings that would 'help the war effort', portraying nothing of the real suffering of the men in the trenches.

It was through this combination of strict censorship and skilfully put-together propaganda campaigns that all possible means of communication were utilised in a unique way to circulate only information that had been 'officially' approved. Civilians on the home front were thus met with these carefully selected facts which aimed to target their sense of honour and pride for their country, making them believe that the war was a worthy success. The wholesale employment of propaganda by both sides during the First World War above all demonstrates that public opinion had become essential to the formulation of war-time government policy, rather than something to be ignored. Morale became a military factor, and the manipulation of public opinion was of supreme importance to success. It was not until much later that the truth of this manipulation became apparent, and when it did it created mistrust and indignation amongst ordinary civilians, who realised that the truth had been wilfully obscured with patriotic slogans and exaggerated reports. It was no surprise that during the Second World War people had to be educated on the very existence of Nazi concentration camps, and convinced that it was not merely more propaganda. The use of propaganda did nevertheless continue, but it developed in sophistication to be an even more direct weapon against the enemy, rather than a tool for promoting support for a war that perhaps was not warranted.

Prologue

Though a lover of peace, Mr. Punch from his earliest days has not been unfamiliar with war. He was born during the Afghan campaign; in his youth England fought side by side with the French, in the Crimea; he saw the old Queen bestow the first Victoria Crosses in 1857; he was moved and stirred by the horrors and heroisms of the Indian Mutiny. A little later on, when our relations with France were strained by the Imperialism of Louis Napoleon, he had witnessed the rise of the volunteer movement and made merry with the activities of the citizen soldier of Brook Green. Later on again he had watched, not without grave misgiving, the growth of the great Prussian war machine which crushed Denmark, overthrew Austria, and having isolated France, overwhelmed her heroic resistance by superior numbers and science, and stripped her of Alsace-Lorraine.

In May, 1864, Mr. Punch presented the King of Prussia with the "Order of St. Gibbet" for his treatment of Denmark.

In August of the same year he portrayed the brigands dividing the spoil and Prussia grabbing the lion's share, thus foreshadowing the inevitable conflict with Austria.

In the war of 1870–1 he showed France on her knees but defying the new Cæsar, and arraigned Bismarck before the altar of Justice for demanding exorbitant securities.

And in 1873, when the German occupation was ended by the payment of the indemnity, in a flash of prophetic vision Mr. Punch pictured France, vanquished but unsubdued, bidding her conqueror "Au revoir."

More than forty years followed, years of peace and prosperity for Great Britain, only broken by the South African war, the wounds of which were healed by a generous settlement. But all the time Germany was preparing for "The Day," steadily perfecting her war machine, enlarging her armies, creating a great fleet, and piling up colossal supplies of guns and munitions, while her professors and historians, harnessed to the car of militarism, inflamed the people against England as the jealous enemy of Germany's legitimate expansion. Abroad, like a great octopus, she was fastening the tentacles of permeation and penetration in every corner of the globe, honeycombing Russia and Belgium, France, England and America with secret agents, spying and intriguing and abusing our hospitality. For twenty-five years the

Above:

GAUL TO THE NEW CÆSAR

"Defiance, Emperor, while I have strength to hurl it!"

(Dec. 17, 1870)

Opposite:

THE REWARD OF (DE)MERIT

King Punch presenteth Prussia with the Order of "St. Gibbet."

(May 7, 1864)

Kaiser was our frequent and honoured, if somewhat embarrassing, guest, professing friendship for England and admiration of her ways, shooting at Sandringham, competing at Cowes, sending telegrams of congratulation to the University boat-race winners, ingratiating himself with all he met by his social gifts, his vivacious conversation, his prodigious versatility and energy.

Mr. Punch was no enemy of Germany. He remembered—none better—the debt we owe to her learning and her art; to Bach and Beethoven, to Handel, the "dear

"Au Revoir!"
Germany: "Farewell, Madam, and if—"
France: "Ha! We shall meet again!"
(Sept. 27, 1873)

Saxon" who adopted our citizenship; to Mendelssohn, who regarded England as his second home; to her fairy tales and folk-lore; to the Brothers Grimm and the *Struwwelpeter*; to the old kindly Germany which has been driven mad by War Lords and Pan-Germans. If Mr. Punch's awakening was gradual he at least recognised the dangerous elements in the Kaiser's character as far back as October, 1888, when he underlined Bismarck's warning against Cæsarism. In March, 1890, appeared Tenniel's famous cartoon "Dropping the Pilot"; in May of the same year the Kaiser appears as the *Enfant Terrible* of Europe, rocking the boat and alarming his fellow-rulers. In January, 1892, he is the Imperial Jack-in-the-Box with a finger in every pie; in March, 1892, the modern Alexander, who

> Assumes the God,
> Affects to nod,
> And seems to shake the spheres;

though unfortunately never nodding in the way that Homer did. (This cartoon, by the way, caused *Punch* to be excluded for a while from the Imperial Palace.)

In February, 1896, Mr. Punch drew the Kaiser as Fidgety Will. In January, 1897, he was the Imperial actor-manager casting himself for a leading part in *Un Voyage en Chine*; in October of the same year he was "Cook's Crusader," sympathising with the Turk at the time of the Cretan ultimatum; and in April, 1903, the famous visit to Tangier suggested the Moor of Potsdam wooing Morocco to the strains of

> "Unter den Linden"—always at Home,
> "Under the Limelight," wherever I roam.

In 1905 the Kaiser was "The Sower of Tares," the enemy of Europe.

In 1910 he was Teutonising and Prussifying Turkey; in 1911 discovering to his discomfort that the Triple Entente was a solid fact.

And in September, 1913, he was shown as unable to dissemble his disappointment at the defeat of the German-trained Turkish army by the Balkan League.

So, too, with Turkey. From 1876 to 1913 Mr. Punch's cartoons on the Near East are one continuous and illuminating commentary on Lord Salisbury's historic admission that we had "backed the wrong horse," culminating in the cartoon "Armageddon: a Diversion" in December, 1912, when Turkey says "Good! If only all these other Christian nations get at one another's throats I may have a dog's chance yet." Throughout the entire series the Sick Man remains cynical and impenitent, blowing endless bubble-promises of reform from his hookah, bullying and massacring his subject races whenever he had the chance, playing off the jealousies of the Powers, one against the other, to further his own sinister ends.

Above:
THE STORY OF FIDGETY WILHELM
(Up-to-date Version of "Struwwelpeter")

"Let me see if Wilhelm can
Be a little gentleman;
Let me see if he is able
To sit still for once at a table!"

"But Fidgety Wil
He *won't* sit still."
Just like any bucking horse.
"Wilhelm! We are getting cross!"

Feb. 1, 1896.

Opposite:
THE SOWER OF TARES
(After Millais, Aug. 23, 1905)

Yet Mr. Punch does not wish to lay claim to any special prescience or wisdom, for, in spite of lucid intervals of foresight, we were all deceived by Germany. Nearly fifty years of peace had blinded us to fifty years of relentless preparation for war. But if we were deceived by the treachery of Germany's false professions, we had no monopoly of illusion. Germany made the huge mistake of believing that we would stand out—that we dared not support France in face of our troubles and divisions at home. She counted on the pacific influences in a Liberal Cabinet, on the loose-

SOLID

Germany: "Donnerwetter! It's rock. I thought it was going to be paper."
(Aug. 2, 1911)

ness of the ties which bound us to our Dominions, on the "contemptible" numbers
of our Expeditionary Force, on the surrender of Belgium. She had willed the War;
the tragedy of Sarajevo gave her the excuse. There is no longer any need to fix the
responsibility. The roots of the world conflict which seemed obscure to a neutral
statesman have long been laid bare by the avowals of the chief criminal. The story
is told in the Memoir of Prince Lichnowsky, in the revelations of Dr. Muehlon of
Krupp's, in the official correspondence that has come to light since the Revolution

of Berlin. Germany stands before the bar of civilisation as the *reus confitens* in the cause of light against darkness, freedom against world enslavement.

So the War began, and if "when war begins then hell opens," the saying gained a tenfold truth in the greatest War of all, when the aggressor at once began to wage it on non-combatants, on the helpless and innocent, on women and children, with a cold and deliberate ferocity unparalleled in history. Let it now be frankly owned that in the shock of this discovery Mr. Punch thought seriously of putting up his shutters. How could he carry on in a shattered and mourning world? The chronicle that follows shows how it became possible, thanks to the temper of all our people in all parts of the Empire, above all to the unwavering confidence of our sailors and soldiers, to that "wonderful spirit of light-heartedness, that perpetual sense of the ridiculous" which, in the words of one of Mr. Punch's many contributors from the front, "even under the most appalling conditions never seemed to desert them, and which indeed seemed to flourish more freely in the mud and rain of the front line trenches than in the comparative comfort of billets or 'cushy jobs.'" Tommy gave Mr. Punch his cue, and his high example was not thrown away on those at home, where, when all allowance is made for shirkers and slackers and scaremongers, callous pleasure seekers, faint-hearted pacificists, rebels and traitors, the great majority so bore themselves as to convince Mr. Punch that it was not only a privilege but a duty to minister to mirth even at times when one hastened to laugh for fear of being obliged to weep. In this resolve he was fortified and encouraged, week after week, by the generous recognition of his efforts which came from all parts of our far-flung line.

This is no formal History of the War in the strict or scientific sense of the phrase; no detailed record of naval and military operations. There have been many occasions on which silence or reticence seemed the only way to maintain the national composure. It is *Mr. Punch's* History of the Great War, a mirror of varying moods, month by month, but reflecting in the main how England remained steadfastly true to her best traditions; how all sorts and conditions of men and women comported themselves throughout the greatest ordeal that had ever befallen their race.

Mr. Punch's History of the Great War

August, 1914.

Four weeks ago we stood on the verge of the great upheaval and knew it not. We were thinking of holidays; of cricket and golf and bathing, and then were suddenly plunged in the deep waters of the greatest of all Wars. It has been a month of rude awakening, of revelation, of discovery—of many moods varying from confidence to deep misgiving, yet dominated by a sense of relief that England has chosen the right course. Sir Edward Grey's statement that we meant to stand by France and fulfil our obligations to Belgium rallied all parties. "Thrice armed is he that hath his quarrel just." The Fleet "stands fast" and the vigil of the North Sea has begun. Lord Kitchener has gone to the War Office and in twelve days from the declaration of War our Expeditionary Force, the best trained and equipped army that England has ever put into the field, landed in France. The Dominions and India are staunch. Every able-bodied public school boy and undergraduate of military age has joined the colours. The Admiralty is crowded with living counterparts of Captain Kettle, offering their services in any capacity, linking up the Merchant Marine with the Royal Navy in one great solidarity of the sea.

The Empire is sound and united. So far the omens are good. But as the days pass the colossal task of the Allies becomes increasingly apparent. Peace-loving nations are confronted by a Power which has prepared for war for forty years, equipped in every detail as no Power has ever been equipped before, with a docile and well-disciplined people trained to arms, fortified by a well-founded belief in their invincibility, reinforced by armies of spies in every country, hostile or neutral. We are up against the mightiest War-machine of all time, wonderful in organisation, joining the savagery of the barbarian to the deadliest resources of modern science. The revelation of the black soul of Germany is the greatest and the most hideous surprise of this month of months, crowning long years of treachery and the abuse of hospitality with an orgy of butchery and devastation—torture and massacre of old men, women and children, the shooting of hostages, the sack and burning of towns and the destruction of ancient seats of learning. Yet we feel that in trampling upon heroic Belgium, who dared to bar the gate, Germany has outraged the conscience of the world and sealed her ultimate doom.

NO THOROUGHFARE

BRAVO, BELGIUM!

The month closes in gloom, the fall of Liège, Namur and Brussels, the sack of Louvain, and the repulse of the Russian raid into East Prussia at Tannenberg following in rapid succession. Against these disasters we have to set the brilliant engagement in the Heligoland Bight. But the onrush of the Germans on the Western front is not stayed, though their timetable has been thrown out by the self-sacrifice of the

Belgians, the steadfast courage of French's "contemptible little army" in the retreat from Mons, and the bold decision of Smith-Dorrien, who saved the situation at Le Cateau. In these days of apprehension and misgiving, clouded by alarming rumours of a broken and annihilated army, it sometimes seems as though we should never smile again. Where, in a world of blood and tears, can *Punch* exercise his function without outraging the fitness of things? These doubts have been with us from the beginning, but they are already being resolved by the discovery—another of the wonders of the time—that on the very fringes of tragedy there is room for cheerfulness. When our fighting men refuse to be downhearted in the direst peril, we at home should follow their high example, note where we can the humours of the fray, and "bear in silence though our hearts may bleed."

Germany in one brief month has given us a wonderful exhibition of conscience-less strength, of disciplined ferocity. She has shown an equally amazing failure to read the character of her foes aright. We now know what German Kultur means: but of the soul and spirit of England she knows nothing. Least of all does she understand that formidable and incorrigible levity which refuses to take hard knocks seriously. It will be our privilege to assist in educating our enemies on these and other points, even though, as Lord Kitchener thinks, it takes three years to do it. The Mad Dog of Europe is loose, but we remember the fate of the dog who "to serve some private ends went mad and bit the man." "The man recovered from his bite, the dog it was that died." Meanwhile the Official Press Bureau has begun its operations, the Prince of Wales's Relief Fund for the relief of those who may suffer distress through the war is started, and in the City

Because beneath grey Northern Skies
    Some grey hulls heave and fall,
The merchants sell their merchandise
      All just as usual.

September, 1914.

Another month of revelations and reticences, of carnage and destruction, loss and gain, with the miracle of the Marne as the first great sign of the turning of the tide. On September 3 the Paris Government moved to Bordeaux, on the 5th the retreat from Mons ended, on the 13th Joffre, always unboastful and laconic, announced the rolling back of the invaders, on the 15th the battle of the Aisne had begun. What an Iliad of agony, endurance and heroism lies behind these dates—the ordeal and deliverance of Paris, the steadfastness of the "Contemptibles," the martyrdom of Belgium!

Medical officer: "Sorry I must reject you on account of your teeth."
Would-be-recruit: "Man, ye're making a gran' mistake. I'm no wanting to bite the Germans, I'm wanting to shoot 'em."

Day by day Germany unmasks herself more clearly in her true colours from highest to lowest. The Kaiser reveals himself as a blasphemer and hypocrite, the Imperial crocodile with the bleeding heart, the Crown Prince as a common brigand, the High Command as chief instigators to ferocity, the rank and file as docile instruments of butchery and torture, content to use Belgian women as a screen when going into action.

The Two Germanies

Marvellous the utter transformation
Of the spirit of the German nation!

Once the land of poets, seers and sages,
Who enchant us in their deathless pages,

Holding high the torch of Truth, and earning
Endless honour by their zeal for learning.

Such the land that in an age uncouther
Bred the soul-emancipating Luther.

Such the land that made our debt the greater
By the gift of *Faust* and *Struwwelpeter*.

Now the creed of Nietzsche, base, unholy,
Guides the nation's brain and guides it solely.

Now Mozart's serene and joyous magic
Yields to Richard Strauss, the hæmorrhagic.*

Now the eagle changing to the vulture
Preaches rapine in the name of culture.

Now the Prussian Junker, blind with fury,
Claims to be God's counsel, judge and jury,

While the authentic German genius slumbers,
Cast into the limbo of back numbers.

The campaign of lies goes on with immense energy in all neutral countries, for the Kaiser is evidently of opinion that the pen is perhaps mightier than the sword.

At home the great improvisation of the New Armies, undertaken by Lord Kitchener in the teeth of much expert criticism, goes steadily on. Lord Kitchener asked for 500,000 men, and he has got them. On September 10 the House voted another half million. The open spaces in Hyde Park are given over to training; women are beginning to take the place of men. Already the spirit of the new soldiers is growing akin to that of the regulars. One of Mr. Punch's brigade, who has begun to send his impressions of the mobilised Territorials, sums it up very well when he says that, amateurs or professionals, they are all very much alike. "Feed them like princes and pamper them like babies, and they'll complain all the time. But stand them up to be shot at and they'll take it as a joke, and rather a good joke, too." Lord Roberts maintains a dignified reticence, but that is "Bobs' way":

He knew, none better, how 'twould be,
    And spoke his warning far and wide:
He worked to save us ceaselessly,
    Setting his well-earned ease aside.

---

* Great play is made in Strauss's *Elektra* with the "slippery blood" motive.

Above:
GOD (AND THE WOMEN) OUR SHIELD
Study of the German Gentleman going into Action

Opposite:
Porter: "Do I know if the Rooshuns has really come to England? Well, sir, if this don't prove
it, I don't know what to do. A train went through here full, and when it came back I knowed
there'd been Rooshuns in it, 'cause the cushions and floors was covered with snow."

We smiled and shrugged and went our way,
  Blind to the swift approaching blow:
His every word proves true to-day,
  But no man hears, "told you so!"

Meanwhile General Botha, Boer and Briton too, is on the war-path, and we can, without an undue stretch of imagination, picture him composing a telegram to the Kaiser in these terms: "Just off to repel another raid. Your customary wire of congratulations should be addressed, 'British Headquarters, German South-West Africa.'"

The rigours of the Censorship are pressing hard on war correspondents. Official news of importance trickles in in driblets: for the rest, newspaper men, miles from the front, are driven to eke out their dispatches with negligible trivialities. We know that Rheims Cathedral is suffering wanton bombardment. And a great many of us believe that at least a quarter of a million Russians have passed through England on their way to France. The number of people who have seen them is large: that of those who have seen people who have seen them is enormous.

We gather that the Press Bureau has no notion whether the rumour is true or not, and cannot think of any way of finding out. But it consents to its publication in the hope that it will frighten the Kaiser. Apropos of the Russians we learn that they have won a pronounced victory (though not by us) at Przemysl.

Motto for the month: *Grattez le Prusse et vous trouverez le barbare.*

UNCONQUERABLE
The Kaiser: "So, you see—you've lost everything."
The King of the Belgians: "Not my soul."

October, 1914.

Antwerp has fallen and the Belgian Government removed to Havre. But the spirit of the King and his army is unshaken.

Unshaken, too, is the courage of Burgomaster Max of Brussels, "who faced the German bullies with the stiffest of stiff backs." The Kaiser has been foiled in his hope of witnessing the fall of Nancy, the drive for the Channel ports has begun at Ypres, and German submarines have retorted to Mr. Churchill's threat to "dig out" the German Fleet "like rats" by torpedoing three battleships. Trench warfare is in full and deadly swing, but "Thomas of the light heart" refuses to be downhearted:

> He takes to fighting as a game,
>   He does no talking through his hat
> Of holy missions: all the same
>   He has his faith—be sure of that:
> He'll not disgrace his sporting breed
>   Nor play what isn't cricket. There's his creed.

Last month Lord Kitchener paid a high tribute to the growing efficiency of the "Terriers" and their readiness to go anywhere. *Punch's* representative with the "Watch Dogs" fully bears out this praise. They have been inoculated and are ready to move on. Some suggest India, others Egypt. "But what tempted the majority was the thought of a season's shooting without having to pay for so much as a gun licence, and so we decided for the Continent."

News from the front continues scanty, and Joffre's laconic *communiqués* might in sum be versified as follows:

> On our left wing the state of things remains
>   Unaltered on a general review,
> Our losses in the centre match our gains,
>   And on our right wing there is nothing new.

Nor do we gain much enlightenment from the "Eyewitness" with G.H.Q., though his literary skill in elegantly describing the things that do not matter moves our admiration.

The Kaiser's sons continue to distinguish themselves as first-class looters, and the ban laid on the English language, including very properly the word "gentleman," has been lifted in favour of Wilhelm Shakespeare.

The prophets are no longer so optimistic in predicting when the War will end. One of Mr. Punch's young men suggests Christmas, 1918. But 500 German prisoners have arrived at Templemore, co. Tipperary. It's a long, long way, but they've got there at last.

THE BULL-DOG BREED

Officer: "Now, my lad, do you know what you are placed here for?"

Recruit: "To prevent the henemy from landin', sir."

Officer: "And do you think you could prevent him landing all by yourself?"

Recruit: "Don't know, sir, I'm sure. But I'd have a damn good try!"

November, 1914.

The miracle of the Marne has been followed by another miracle—that of Ypres. Outgunned and outnumbered, our thin line has stemmed the rush to the sea.

The road to Calais has been blocked like that to Paris. Heartening news comes from afar of the fall of Tsing-tau before our redoubtable Japanese allies, and with it the crumbling of Germany's scheme of an Oriental Empire; of the British occupation of Basra; and of the sinking of the *Emden*, thanks to the "good hunting" of the *Sydney*—first fruits of Australian aid. A new enemy has appeared in Turkey, but her defection has its consolations. It is something to be rid of an "unspeakable" incubus full of promises of reform never fulfilled, "sick" but unrepentant, always turning European discord to bloody account at the expense of her subject nationalities: in all respects a fitting partner for her ally and master.

At sea our pain at the loss of the *Good Hope* and *Monmouth* off Coronel is less than our pride in the spirit of the heroic Cradock, true descendant of Grenville and Nelson, prompt to give battle against overwhelming odds. The soul of the "Navy Eternal" draws fresh strength from his example. So, too, does the Army from the death of Lord Roberts, the "happy warrior," who passed away while visiting the Western front. The best homage we can pay him is not grief or

> Vain regret for counsel given in vain,
> But service of our lives to keep her free
>   The land he served: a pledge above his grave
> To give her even such a gift as he,
>   The soul of loyalty, gave.

Even the Germans have paid reluctant tribute to one who, as Bonar Law said in the House, "was in real life all, and more than all, that Colonel Newcome was in fiction." He was the exemplar *in excelsis* of those "bantams," "little and good," who, after being rejected for their diminutive stature, are now joining up under the new regulations:

> Apparently he's just as small,
>   But since his size no more impedes him
> In spirit he is six foot tall—
>   Because his country needs him.

We have begun to think in millions. The war is costing a million a day. The Chancellor of the Exchequer has launched a war loan of 230 millions and doubled our income tax. The Prime Minister asks for an addition of a million men to the Regular Army. But the country has not yet fully awakened to the realities of war. Football clubs are concerned with the "jostling of the ordinary patrons" by men in uniform. "Business as usual" is interpreted as "pleasure as usual" in some quarters. Rumour is busy with stories of mysterious prisoners in the Tower, with tales of huge guns which are to shell us from Calais when the Germans get there; with reports (from neutral sources) of the speedy advent of scores of Zeppelins and hundreds of aeroplanes over London. But though

> Old England's dark o' nights and short
>   Of 'buses: still she's much the sort
> Of place we always used to know.

It is otherwise with Belgium, with its shattered homes and wrecked towns. The great Russian legend is still going strong, in spite of the statements of the Under-Secretary for War, and, after all, why should the Germans do all the story telling? By the way, a "German Truth Society" has been founded. It is pleasant to know that it is realised over there at last that there is a difference between Truth and German Truth. The British Navy, we learn from the *Kölnische Zeitung*, "is in hiding." But our fragrant contemporary need not worry. In due course the Germans shall have the hiding.

THE EXCURSIONIST

Tripper Wilhelm: "First Class to Paris."

Clerk: "Line blocked."

Wilhelm: "Then make it Warsaw."

Clerk: "Line blocked."

Wilhelm: "Well, what about Calais?"

Clerk: "Line blocked."

Wilhelm: "Hang it! I *must* go *somewhere!* I promised my people I would."

T.B.D

Officer's Steward: "Will you take your bath sir, before or after haction?"

In some ways the unchanged spirit of our people is rather disconcerting. One of Mr. Punch's young men, happening to meet a music-hall acquaintance, asked him how he thought the war was going, and met with the answer: "Oh, I think the managers will have to give in." And the proposal to change the name of Berlin Road at Lewisham has been rejected by the residents.

December, 1914.

In less than six weeks Coronel has been avenged at the battle of the Falkland Islands:

> Hardened steel are our ships;
>   Gallant tars are our men;
> We never are wordy
>   (STURDEE, boys, STURDEE!),
> But quietly conquer again and again.

Here at least we can salute the vanquished. Admiral von Spee, who went down with his doomed squadron, was a gallant and chivalrous antagonist, like Captain Müller, of the *Emden*. Germany's retort, eight days later, by bombarding Scarborough and Whitby, reveals the normal Hun:

> Come where you will—the seas are wide;
>   And choose your Day—they're all alike;
> You'll find us ready when we ride
>   In calm or storm and wait to strike;
> But—if of shame your shameless Huns
>   Can yet retrieve some casual traces—
> Please fight our men and ships and guns,
>   Not womenfolk and watering places.

Austria's "punitive expedition" has ended in disaster for the Austrians. They entered Belgrade on the 2nd, and were driven out twelve days later by the Serbs. King George has paid his first visit to the front, and made General Foch a G.C.B. We know that the General is a great authority on strategy, and that his name, correctly pronounced, rhymes with Boche, as hero with Nero. He is evidently a man likely to be heard of again. Another hitherto unfamiliar name that has cropped up is that of Herr Lissauer, who, for writing a "Hymn of Hate" against England, has been decorated by the Kaiser. This shows true magnanimity on the part of the Kaiser, in his capacity of King of Prussia, since the "Hymn of Hate" turns out to be a close adaptation of a poem composed by a Saxon patriot, in which Prussia, not England, was held up to execration.

Kitchener's great improvisation is already bearing fruit, and the New Armies are flocking to the support of the old. Indian troops are fighting gallantly in three continents. King Albert "the unconquerable," in the narrow strip of his country that still belongs to him, waits in unshaken faith for the coming of the dawn. And as Christmas draws on the thoughts of officers and men in the waterlogged trenches turn fondly homeward to mothers, wives and sweethearts:

Cheer up! I'm calling far away;
    And wireless you can hear.
Cheer up! You know you'd have me stay
    And keep on trying day by day;
We're winning, never fear.

Christmas at least brings the children's truce, and that is something to be thankful for, but it is not the Christmas that we knew and long for:

On Earth—Peace

No stir of wings sweeps softly by;
    No angel comes with blinding light;
Beneath the wild and wintry sky
    No shepherds watch their flocks to-night.

In the dull thunder of the wind
    We hear the cruel guns afar,
But in the glowering heavens we find
    No guiding, solitary star.

But lo! on this our Lord's birthday,
    Lit by the glory whence she came,
Peace, like a warrior, stands at bay,
    A swift, defiant, living flame!

Full-armed she stands in shining mail,
    Erect, serene, unfaltering still,
Shod with a strength that cannot fail,
    Strong with a fierce o'ermastering will.

Above:

THE CHILDREN'S PEACE

Peace: "I'm glad that they, at least, have their Christmas unspoiled."

Opposite:

Pompous Lady: "I shall descend at Knightsbridge."
Tommy (aside): "Takes 'erself for a bloomin' Zeppelin!"

Where shattered homes and ruins be
   She fights through dark and desperate days;
Beside the watchers on the sea
   She guards the Channel's narrow ways.

Through iron hail and shattering shell,
   Where the dull earth is stained with red,
Fearless she fronts the gates of Hell
   And shields the unforgotten dead.

So stands she, with her all at stake,
   And battles for her own dear life,
That by one victory she may make
   For evermore an end of strife.

Yet we have our minor war gains in the temporary disappearance of cranks and faddists, some of whom have sunk without a ripple. And though the Press Censor's suppressions and delays and inconsistencies provoke discontent in the House and out of it, food for mirth turns up constantly in unexpected quarters. The Crown

Prince tells an American interviewer that there is no War Party in Germany, nor has there ever been. The German General Staff have begun to disguise set-backs under the convenient euphemism that the situation has developed "according to expectation." An English village worthy, discussing the prospects of invasion, comes to the reassuring conclusion that "there can't be no battle in these parts, Jarge, for there bain't no field suitable, as you may say; an' Squire, 'e won't lend 'em the use of 'is park." The troubles of neutrality are neatly summed up in a paper in a recent geography examination. "Holland is a low country, in fact it is such a very low country that it is no wonder that it is dammed all round."

The trials of mistresses on the home front are happily described in the reply of a child to a small visitor who inquired after her mother. "Thank you, poor mummie's a bit below herself this morning—what with the cook and the Kaiser."

We have to thank an ingenious Correspondent for drawing up the following "credibility index" for the guidance of perplexed newspaper readers:

London, Paris, or Petrograd (official)	100
" " " (semi-official)	50
Berlin (official)	25
It is believed in military circles here that—	24
A correspondent that has just returned from the firing-line tells me that—	18
Our correspondent at Rome announces that—	11
Berlin (unofficial)	10
I learn from a neutral merchant that—	7
A story is current in Venice to the effect that—	5
It is rumoured that—	4
I have heard to-day from a reliable source that—	3
I learn on unassailable authority that—	2
It is rumoured in Rotterdam that—	1
Wolff's Bureau states that—	0

January, 1915.

General von Kluck "never got round on the right." Calais is Calais still, and the Kaiser, if he still wishes to give it a new name, may call it the "Never, Never Land." "General Janvier" is doing his worst, but our men are sticking it out through slush and slime. As for the Christmas truce and fraternisation, the British officer who ended a situation that was proving impossible by presenting a dingy Saxon with a copy of *Punch* in exchange for a packet of cigarettes, acted with a wise candour:

For there he found, our dingy friend,
    Amid the trench's sobering slosh,
What must have left him, by the end,
    A wiser, if a sadder, Boche,
Seeing himself, with chastened mien,
In that pellucid well of Truth serene.

There can be no "fraternising" with Fritz until he realises that he has been fooled by his War Lords; and his awakening is a long way off. Lord Kitchener has been charged with being "very economical in his information" vouchsafed to the Lords, but it is well to be rid of illusions. This has not been a month of great events. General Joffre is content with this ceaseless "nibbling." The Kaiser, nourished by the flattery of his tame professors, encourages the war on non-combatants.

The Turks are beginning to show a gift for euphemism in disguising their reverses in the Caucasus, which shows that they have nothing to learn from their masters; Austria, badly mauled by the Serbians, addresses awful threats to Roumania; and the United States has issued a warning Note on neutral trading. But the American Eagle is not the Eagle that we are up against.

The number of Mr. Punch's correspondents on active service steadily grows. Some of them are at the Western front; others are still straining at the leash at home; another of the *Punch* brigade, with the very first battalion of Territorials to land in India, has begun to send his impressions of the shiny land; of friendly natives and unfriendly ants; of the disappointment of being relegated to clerical duties instead of going to the front; of the evaporation of visions of military glory in the routine of typing, telephoning and telegraphing; of leisurely Oriental methods. Being a soldier clerk in India is very different from being a civilian clerk in England. Patience, good Territorials in India, your time will come.

At home, though the "knut" has been commandeered and nobly transmogrified, though women are increasingly occupied in war work and entering with devotion and self-sacrifice on their new duties as substitutes for men, we have not yet been wholly purged of levity and selfishness. Football news has not receded into its true perspective; shirkers are more preoccupied with the defeat or victory of "Lambs" or "Wolves" in Lancashire than with the stubborn defence, the infinite discomfort and the heavy losses of their brothers in Flanders.

Overdressed fashionables pester wounded officers and men with their unreasonable visits and futile queries. The enemies in our midst are not all aliens; there are not a few natives we should like to see interned.

The Kaiser has had his first War birthday and, as the Prussian Government has ordered that there shall be no public celebrations, this confirms the rumours that he now wishes he had never been born.

THE FLIGHT THAT FAILED

The Emperor: "What! No babes, Sirrah?"

The Murderer: "Alas, Sire, none."

The Emperor: "Well, then, no babes, no iron crosses."

(*Exit murderer, discouraged.*)

THE SHIRKERS' WAR NEWS
"There! What did I tell you? Northdown Lambs beaten—two to nothing."

Germany, says the *Cologne Gazette* in an article on the food question, "has still at hand a very large supply of pigs"—even after the enormous number she has exported to Belgium. Germany, however, does not only export pigs; her trade in "canards" with neutrals grows and grows, chiefly with the United States, thanks to the untiring mendacity of Bernstorff and Wolff. Compared with these efforts, the revelations of English governesses at German courts, which are now finding their way into print, make but a poor show.

As the British armies increase, the moustache of the British officer, one of the most astonishing products of these astonishing times, grows "small by degrees and beautifully less." Waxed ends, fashionable in a previous generation, are now only worn by policemen, taxi-drivers and labour leaders. The Kaiser remains faithful to the Mephistophelean form. But in proof of his desire to make the best of both worlds, nether and celestial, he continues to commandeer "Gott" on every occasion as his second in command. Out-Heroding Herod as a murderer of innocents, he enters into a competition of piety with his grandfather. For we should not forget that the first German Emperor's messages to his wife in the Franco-Prussian War were once summed up by Mr. Punch:

Ten thousand French have gone below;
Praise God from Whom all blessings flow.

February, 1915.

January ended with a knock for the Germans off the Dogger Bank, when the *Blücher* was sunk by our Battle-Cruiser Squadron:

> They say the *Lion* and the *Tiger* sweep
> Where once the Huns shelled babies from the deep,
> And *Blücher*, that great cruiser—12-inch guns
> Roar o'er his head, but cannot break his sleep.

And now it is the turn of "Johnny Turk," who has had *his* knock on the Suez Canal, and failed to solve the *Riddle of the Sands* under German guidance. Having safely locked up his High Seas Fleet in the Kiel Canal, the Kaiser has ordered the U-boat blockade of England to begin by the torpedoing of neutral as well as enemy merchant ships.

You may know a man by the company he keeps, and the Kaiser's friends are now the Jolly Roger and Sir Roger Casement.

Valentine's Day has come and gone. Here are some lines from a damp but undefeated lover in the trenches:

> Though the glittering knight whose charger
>   Bore him on his lady's quest
> With an infinitely larger
>   Share of warfare's pomp was blest,
> Yet he offered love no higher,
>   No more difficult to quench,
> Than the filthy occupier
>   Of this unromantic trench.

The fusion of classes in the camps of the New Armies outdoes the mixture of "cook's son and duke's son" fifteen years ago. The old Universities are now given up to a handful of coloured students, Rhodes' scholars and reluctant crocks. As a set-off, however, a Swansea clergyman and football enthusiast has held a "thanksgiving service for their good fortune against Newcastle United." Meanwhile, the Under-Secretary for War has stated that the army costs more in a week than the total estimates for the Waterloo campaign, and that our casualties in the Western front alone have amounted to over 100,000. So what with submarine losses, ubiquitous German spies, the German propaganda in America, and complaints of Government inactivity, the pessimists are having a fine time. Tommy grouses of course, but then he complains far more of the loss of a packet of cigarettes or a tin of peppermints or a mouth-organ than of the loss of a limb.

RUNNING AMOK
German Bull: "I know I'm making a rotten exhibition of myself; but I shall tell everybody I was goaded into it."

Germany's attitude towards the United States tempers the blandishments of the serenader with the occasional discharge of half-bricks. There is no such inconsistency in the expression of her feelings about England. Articles entitled *"Unser Hass gegen England"* constantly appear in the German Press, and people are beginning to wonder whether the *Hass* is not the Kaiser. Apropos of newspapers, we are beginning to harbour a certain envy of the Americans. Even their provincial organs often contain important and cheering news of the doings of the British Army many days before the Censor releases the information in England. Daylight saving is again being talked of, and it would surely be an enormous boon to rush the measure through now so that the Germans may have less darkness of which to take advantage. And there is a general and reasonable feeling that more use should be made of bands for recruiting. The ways of German musicians are perplexing. Here is the amiable Herr Humperdinck, composer of "Hänsel and Gretel," the very embodiment of the old German kindliness, signing the Manifesto of patriotic artists and professors who execrate England, while Strauss, the truculent "Mad Mullah" of the Art, holds aloof. Dr. Hans Richter, who enjoyed English hospitality so long, now clamours for our extinction; it is even said that he has asked to be allowed to conduct a *Parsifal* airship to this country.

March, 1915.

A new and possibly momentous chapter has opened in the history of the War by the attempt to force the Dardanelles. At the end of February the Allied Fleet bombarded the forts at the entrance, and landed a party of bluejackets. Since then these naval operations have been resumed, and our new crack battleship *Queen Elizabeth* has joined in the attack. We have not got through the Narrows, and some sceptical critics are asking what we should do if we got through to Constantinople, without a land force. It is a great scheme, if it comes off; and the "only begetter" of it, if report is true, is Mr. Winston Churchill, the strategist of the Antwerp expedition, who now aspires to be the Dardanelson of our age. Anyhow, the Sultan, lured on by the Imperial William o' the Wisp, is already capable of envying even his predecessor:

> Abdul! I would that I had shared your plight,
>   Or Europe seen my heels,
> Before the hour when Allah bound me tight
>   To WILLIAM's chariot-wheels!

Germany, always generous with other people's property, has begun to hint to Italy possibilities of compensation in the shape of certain portions of Austro-Hungarian territory. She has also declared that she is "fighting for the independence of the small nations," including, of course, Belgium. In further evidence of her humanity she has taken to spraying our soldiers in the West with flaming petrol and squirting boiling pitch over our Russian allies. It is positively a desecration of the word devil to apply it to the Germans whether on land, on or under water, or in the air.

STUDY OF A PRUSSIAN HOUSEHOLD HAVING ITS MORNING HATE

We have begun to "push" on the Western front, and Neuve Chapelle has been captured, after a fierce battle and at terrible cost. Air raids are becoming common in East Anglia and U-boats unpleasantly active in the North Sea. Let us take off our hats to the mine-sweepers and trawlers, the new and splendid auxiliaries of the Royal Navy. Grimsby is indeed a "name to resound for ages" for what its fishermen have done and are doing in the war against mine and submarine:

Soles in the Silver Pit—an' there we'll let 'em lie;
Cod on the Dogger—oh, we'll fetch 'em by an' by;
War on the water—an' it's time to serve an' die,
    For there's wild work doin' on the North Sea ground.
An' it's "Wake up, Johnnie" they want you at the trawlin'
(With your long sea-boots and your tarry old tarpaulin);
All across the bitter seas duty comes a-callin'
    In the Winter's weather off the North Sea ground.
It's well we've learned to laugh at fear—the sea has taught us how;
It's well we've shaken hands with death—we'll not be strangers now,
With death in every climbin' wave before the trawler's bow,
    An' the black spawn swimmin' on the North Sea ground.

These brave men and their heroic brothers in the trenches are true sportsmen as well as patriots, not those who interpret the need of lightheartedness by the cult of "sport as usual" on the football field and the racecourse. And the example of the Universities shines with the same splendour. Of the scanty remnant that remain at Oxford and Cambridge all the physically fit have joined the O.T.C. Boat-race day has passed, but the crews are gone to "keep it long" and "pull it through" elsewhere:

Not here their hour of great emprise;
    No mounting cheer towards Mortlake roars;
Lulled to full tide the river lies
    Unfretted by the fighting oars;
The long high toil of strenuous play
    Serves England elsewhere well to-day.

London changes daily. The sight of the female Jehu is becoming familiar; the lake in St. James's Park has been drained and the water-fowl driven to form a concentration camp by the sorry pool that remains beside the Whitehall Gate.

Spy-hunting is prevalent in East Anglia, but the amateurs have not achieved any convincing results. Spring poets are suffering from suspended animation; there is a slump in

WILLIAM O' THE WISP

crocuses, snowdrops, daffodils and lambkins. Their "musings always turn away to men who're arming for the fray." The clarion and the fife have ousted the pastoral ode. And our military and naval experts, harassed by the Censor, take refuge in psychology.

The *Kölnische Zeitung* has published a whole article on "Mr. Punch." The writer, a Herr Professor, finds our cartoons lacking in "modest refinement." Indeed, he goes so far as to say that the treatment of the Kaiser savours of blasphemy. One is so apt to forget that the Kaiser is a divinity, so prone to remember that Luther wrote, "We Germans are Germans, and Germans we will remain—that is to say, pigs and brutish animals." This was written in 1528: but "the example of the Middle Ages" is held up to-day by German leaders as the true fount of inspiration.

April, 1915.

A hundred years ago Bismarck was born on April 1, the man who built with blood and iron, but now only the blood remains. Yet one may doubt whether even that strong and ruthless pilot would have commended the submarine crew who sank the liner *Falaba* and laughed at the cries and struggles of drowning men and women. Sooner or later these crews are doomed to die the death of rats:

> But you, who sent them out to do this shame;
>   From whom they take their orders and their pay;
> For you—avenging wrath defers its claim,
>   And Justice bides her day.

The tide of "frightfulness" rolls strong on land as on sea. The second battle of Ypres has begun and the enemy has resorted to the use of a new weapon—poison gas. He had already poisoned wells in South-West Africa, but this is an uglier outcome of the harnessing of science to the Powers of Darkness. Italy grows restive in spite of the blandishments of Prince Bülow, and as the month closes we hear of the landing of the Allies in Gallipoli, just two months after the unsupported naval attempt to force the Dardanelles. British and Australian and New Zealand troops have achieved the impossible by incredible valour in face of murderous fire, and a foothold has been won at tremendous cost of heroic lives. Letters from the Western front continue cheerful, but it does not need much reading between the lines to realise the odds with which our officers and men have to contend, the endless discomfort and unending din. They are masters of a gallant art of metaphor which belittles the most appalling horrors of trench warfare; masters, too, of the art of extracting humorous relief from the most trivial incidents.

On the home front we have to contend with a dangerous ally of the enemy in Drink, and with the self-advertising politicians who do their bit by asking unnecessary questions. Sometimes, but rarely, they succeed in eliciting valuable information, as in Mr. Lloyd George's statement on the situation at the front. We have now six times as many

THE WAR SPIRIT AT THE BRITISH MUSEUM
Ardent Egyptologist (who has lately joined the Civic Guard): "No. I seem to have lost my enthusiasm for this group since I noticed Bes-Hathor-Horus was out of step with the other two."

men in the field as formed the original Expeditionary Force, and in the few days fighting round Neuve Chapelle almost as much ammunition was expended by our guns as in the whole of the two and three-quarter years of the Boer War.

The Kaiser has been presented with another grandson, but it has not been broken to the poor little fellow who he is. It is also reported that the Kaiser has bestowed an Iron Cross on a learned pig—one of a very numerous class.

May, 1915.

We often think that we must have got to the end of German "frightfulness," only to have our illusions promptly shattered by some fresh and amazing explosion of calculated ferocity. Last month it was poison gas; now it is the sinking of the *Lusitania*.

Above:
THE HAUNTED SHIP
Ghost of the Old Pilot: "I wonder if he would drop me *now!*"

Opposite:
AN OMEN OF 1908
Reproduced from "Christmas Cards for Celebrities," in *Mr. Punch's Almanack* of that year.

Yet Mr. Punch had read the omens, some seven and a half years ago, when the records established by that liner had created a jealousy in Germany which the Kaiser and his agents have now appeased, but at what a cost! The House of Commons is an odd place, unique in its characteristics. Looking round the benches when it reassembled on May 10th, and noting the tone and purport of the inquiries addressed to the First Lord, one might well suppose that nothing remarkable had happened since Parliament adjourned. The questions were numerous but all practical, and as unemotional as if they referred to outrages by a newly-discovered race of fiends in human shape peopling Mars or Saturn. The First Lord, equally undemonstrative, announced that the Board of Trade have ordered an inquiry into the circumstances attending the disaster. Pending the result, it would be premature to discuss the matter. Here we have the sublimation of officialism and national phlegm. Of the 1,200 victims who went down in this unarmed passenger ship about 200 were Americans. What will America say or do?

> In silence you have looked on felon blows,
>   On butcher's work of which the waste lands reek!
> Now in God's name, from Whom your greatness flows,
>   Sister, will you not speak?

Many unofficial voices have been raised in horror, indignation, and even in loud calls for intervention. The leaven works, but President Wilson, though not unmoved, gives little sign of abandoning his philosophic neutrality.

In Europe it is otherwise. Italy has declared war on Austria; her people have driven the Government to take the path of freedom and honour and break the shackles of Germanism in finance, commerce and politics.

Italy has not declared war on Germany yet, but the fury of the German Press is unbounded, and for the moment Germany's overworked Professors of Hate have focused their energies on the new enemy, and its army of "vagabonds, convicts, ruffians and mandolin-players," conveniently forgetting that the spirit of Garibaldi is still an animating force, and that the King inherits the determination of his grandfather and namesake.

On the Western front the enemy has been repulsed at Ypres. Lord Kitchener has asked for another 300,000 men, and speaks confidently of our soon being able to make good the shortage of ammunition.

On the Eastern front the Grand Duke Nicholas has been forced to give ground; in Gallipoli slow progress is being made at heavy cost on land and sea. The Turk is a redoubtable trench fighter and sniper; the difficulties of the *terrain* are indescribable, yet our men continue the epic struggle with unabated heroism. King Constantine of Greece, improved in health, construes his neutrality in terms of ever increasing benevolence to his brother-in-law the Kaiser.

HAMLET U.S.A
Scene: The Ramparts of the White House
President Wilson: "The time is out of joint, O cursed spite,
That ever I was born to set it right!"
Voice of Roosevelt (*off*): "That's so!"

THE REWARD OF KULTUR

At home the great event has been the formation of a Coalition Government—a two-handed sword, as we hope, to smite the enemy; while practical people regard it rather as a "Coal and Ammunition Government." The cost of the War is now Two Millions a day, and a new campaign of Posters and Publicity has been inaugurated to promote recruiting. Volunteers, with scant official recognition, continue their training on foot; the Hurst Park brigade continue their activities, mainly on rubber wheels. An evening paper announces:

Victory in Gallipoli.
Late wire from Chester.

Mr. Punch is prompted to comment:

For these our Army does its bit,
    While they in turn peruse
Death's honour-roll (should time permit)
    After the Betting News.

More agreeable is the sportsmanship of the trenches, where a correspondent tells of the shooting of a hare and the recovery of the corpse, by a reckless Tommy, from the turnip-field which separated our trenches from those of Fritz.

Amongst other signs of the times the emergence of the Spy Play is to be noted, in which the alien enemy within our gates is gloriously confounded. Yet, if a certain Section of the Press is to be believed, the dark and sinister operations of the Hidden Hand continue unchecked.

The Germans as unconscious humorists maintain their supremacy *hors concours.* A correspondent of the *Cologne Gazette* was with other journalists recently entertained to dinner in a French villa by the Crown Prince Rupprecht of Bavaria. "The party, while dining," we are told, "talked of the defects of French taste, and Prince Rupprecht said that French houses were full of horrors." True, O Prince, but the French are determined to drive them out. Better still, in the month which witnessed the sinking of the *Lusitania* we read this panegyric of the Teuton in *Die Welt:* "Clad in virtue and in peerless nobility of character, unassailed by insidious enemies either within or without, girded about by the benign influences of Kultur, the German, whether soldier or civilian, pursues his destined way, fearless and serene."

June, 1915.

The weeks that have passed since the sinking of the *Lusitania* have left Germany not merely impenitent but glorying in her crime. "The destruction of the *Lusitania*," says Herr Baumgarten, Professor of Theology, "should be greeted with jubilation and enthusiastic cheering, and everybody who does not cheer is no real or true German." Many harsh things have been said of the Germans, but nothing quite so bitter as this suggestion for a test of nationality. But while Germany jubilates, her Government is painfully anxious to explain everything to the satisfaction of America. The conversations between the two Powers are continuous but abortive. President Wilson's dove has returned to him, with the report "Nothing doing," and the American eagle looks as if he would like to take on the job.

Germany has had her first taste of real retaliation in the bombardment of Karlsruhe by Allied airmen, and is furiously indignant at the attack on an "unfortified and peaceful" town— which happens to be the headquarters of the 14th German Army Corps and to contain an important arsenal as well as large chemical, engineering and railway works. Also she is very angry with Mr. Punch, and has honoured him and other British papers with a solemn warning. Our performances, it seems, are "diligently noted, so that when the day of reckoning arrives we shall know with whom we have to deal, and how to deal with them effectually." It is evident that in spite of Italy's entry into the war the mass of the Germans are still true to their old hate of England.

But Germany does not merely talk. She has been indulging in drastic reprisals in consequence of Mr. Winston Churchill's memorandum on the captured submarine crews. As a result 39 imprisoned British officers, carefully selected, have been subjected to solitary confinement under distressing conditions in return for Mr. Churchill's having hinted at possible severities which were never carried out. Moral: Do not threaten unless you mean to act. The retirement of Mr. Churchill to the seclusion of the Duchy of Lancaster and the appointment of Mr. Balfour to the First Lordship of the Admiralty afford hope that the release of the Thirty-Nine from their special hardship will not be unduly postponed. The Coalition Government is shaking down. A Ministry of Munitions has been created, with Mr. Lloyd George in charge; and members of the Cabinet have decided to pool their salaries with a view to their being divided equally. Mr. McKenna has made his first appearance as Chancellor of the Exchequer and introduced a Bill authorising the raising of a War Loan unlimited in extent, but, being a man of moderate views, will be satisfied if nine hundred millions are forthcoming. Lord Haldane has been succeeded in the Lord Chancellorship by Lord Buckmaster, having caused by one unfortunate phrase a complete oblivion of all the services rendered by his creation of the Territorial system. The cry for "more men" has now changed to one for "more shells," and certain newspapers, always in search of a scapegoat, have entered on a campaign directed against Lord Kitchener, the very man whom a few short months ago they hailed as the saviour of the situation. Finding that the public cannot live on their hot air, they are doing their best to make our flesh creep and keep our feet cold. Let us hope that K. of K. will find the Garter some slight protection against this hitting below the belt.

On the Black List

Kaiser (as executioner): "I'm going to hang you."

Punch: "Oh you are, are you? Well, you don't seem to know how this scene ends. It's the hangman that gets hanged."

SOME BIRD

The Returning Dove (to President Woodrow Noah): "Nothing doing."

The Eagle: "Say, Boss, what's the matter with trying me?"

The Russian retreat continues, but there is no *débâcle*. Greece shows signs of returning sanity in the restoration to power of her one strong man, M. Venizelos. If there were a few more like him then (to adapt Porson) "the Germanised Greek would be sadly to seek." As it is, he flourishes exceedingly, under the patronage of a Prussianised Court.

In Gallipoli the deadly struggle goes on; our foothold has been strengthened by bitter fighting and our lines pushed forward for three miles by a few hundred yards—a big advance in modern trench warfare. Blazing heat and a plague of flies add to the discomforts of our men, but a new glory has been added to the ever growing vocabulary of the war in "Anzac." There is a lull on the Western front, if such a word properly can be applied to the ceaseless activities of the war of position, of daily *strafe* and counter-*strafe*.

At home, khaki weddings are becoming common form. By an inversion of the old order the bride is now eclipsed by the bridegroom:

'Tis well: the lack of fine array
    Best fits a sacrificial altar;
Her man to-morrow joins the fray,
    And yet she does not falter;
Simple her gown, but still we see
The bride in all her bravery.

Society is losing much of its snap through the political truce. It is all very well to talk of the lion lying down with the lamb, but of course it makes life a distinctly duller business both for the lion and the lamb when each has lost his or her dearest enemy. For the rest, there is a brisk trade in anti-gas respirators, "lonely soldiers" are becoming victimised by fair correspondents, and a new day has been added to the week—flag day.

Proverb for the month, suggested by the activities of the Imperial infanticide: "The hand that wrecks the cradle rules the world."

July, 1915.

The last month of the first year of the war brings no promise of a speedy end; it is not a month of great battles on land or sea, but rather of omens and foreshadowings, good and evil. To the omens of victory belongs the sinking of the *Pommern*, named after the great maritime province, so long coveted by the Brandenburgers, the makers of Prussia and the true begetters of Prussianism. Of good omen, too, has been the "clean sweep" made by General Botha in German South-West Africa,

First trawler skipper (to friend who is due to sail by next tide): "Are ye takin' any precautions against these submarines, Jock?"
Second skipper: "Ay! Although I've been in the habit o' carryin' my bits of bawbees wi' me, I went an bankit them this mornin', an' I'm no taking ma best oilskins or ma new seaboots."
First Skipper: Oh. *you're* a'richt, then. Ye'll hae practically nothin' tae lose but yer life."

where the enemy surrendered unconditionally on July 9. And though the menace of the U-boat grows daily, there *may* be limits to America's seemingly inexhaustible forbearance. There are happily none to the fortitude of our bluejackets and trawlers.

Pundits in the Press, fortified by warnings from generals in various Home Commands, display an increasing preoccupation with the likelihood of invasion by sea. Mr. Punch naturally inclines to a sceptical attitude, swayed by long adherence to the views of the Blue Water School and the incredulousness of correspondents engaged in guarding likely spots on the East Coast. With runaway raids by sea we are already acquainted, and their growing frequency from the air is responsible for various suggested precautions, official and otherwise—pails of sand and masks and anti-asphyxiation mixtures—which are not viewed with much sympathy in the trenches. *There* the men meet the most disconcerting situations—as, for example, the problem of spending a night in a flooded meadow occupied by a thunderstorm—with irrelevant songs or fantasias on the mouth-organ.

> Oh, there ain't no band to cheer us up, there ain't no Highland pipers
> To keep our warlike ardure warm round New Chapelle and Wipers,
> So—since there's nothing like a tune to glad the 'eart o' man,
> Why Billy with his mouth-organ 'e does the best 'e can.

> Wet, 'ungry, thirsty, 'ot or cold, whatever may betide 'im,
> 'E'll play upon the 'ob of 'ell while the breath is left inside 'im;
> And when we march up Potsdam Street, and goose-step through Berlin,
> Why Billy with 'is mouth-organ 'e'll play the Army in!

When officers come home on leave and find England standing where she did, their views support the weather-beaten major who said that it was "worth going to a little trouble and expense to keep that intact." But you can hardly expect people who live in trenches which have had to be rebuilt twice daily for the last few months and are shelled at all hours of the day or night, to compassionate the occasional trials of the home-keeping bomb-dodger. The war, as it goes on, seems to bring out the best and the worst that is in us. South Wales responded loyally to the call for recruits, yet 200,000 miners are affected by the strike fever.

The House, where party strife for a brief space was hushed by mutual consent, is now devastated by the energies of indiscreet, importunate, egotistic or frankly disloyal question-mongers. We want a censorship of Parliamentary Reports. The Press Bureau withholds records of shining courage at the front lest they should enlighten the enemy, but gives full publicity to those

> Who give us words in lieu of deeds,
> Content to blather while their country bleeds.

There is, however, some excuse for those importunates who wish to know on what authority the Premier declared at Newcastle that neither our Allies nor ourselves have been hampered by an insufficient supply of munitions. In two months' fighting in Gallipoli our casualties have largely exceeded those sustained by us during the whole of the Boer War. And financial purists may be pardoned for their protests against extravagant expenditure in view of the announcement that the war is now costing well over three millions daily. The idea of National Registration has taken shape in a Bill, which has passed its second reading,. The notion of finding out what everyone can do to help his country in her hour of need is excellent. But the

THE OLD MAN OF THE SEA

Sinbad the Kaiser: "This submarine business is going to get me into trouble with America; but what can an All-powerful do with a thing like this on his back?"

Government do not seem to have realised that half a million volunteer soldiers have been waiting and ready for a job for the last six months:

And when at last you come and say
   "What can you do? We ask for light
On any service you can pay,"
   The answer is: "*You* know all right,
And all this weary while you knew it;
The trouble was you wouldn't let us do it"

The German Press is not exactly the place where one expects to find occasion for merriment. Yet listen to this from the *Neueste Nachrichten*: "Our foes ask themselves continuously, How can we best get at Germany's vital parts? What are her most vulnerable points? The answer is, her humanity—her trustful honesty." Here, on the other hand, thousands of people, by knocking months and years off their real age, have been telling good straightforward lies for their country. At the Front euphemism in describing hardship is mingled with circumlocution in official terminology. Thus one C.O. is reported to refer to the enemy not as Germans but "militant bodies of composite Teutonic origin."

A new and effectual cure for the conversion of pessimists at home has been discovered. It is simply to out-do the prophets of ill at their own game. The result is that they seek you out to tell you that a enemy submarine has been sunk off the Scillies or that the Crown Prince is in the Tower. It is the old story that optimists are those who have been associating with pessimists and *vice versa*. But seriousness is spreading. We are told that even actresses are now being photographed with their mouths shut, though one would have thought that at such a time all British subjects—especially the "Odolisques" of the variety stage—ought to show their teeth.

August, 1915.

Ordinary anniversaries lead to retrospect: after a year of the greatest of all wars it is natural to indulge in a stock-taking of the national spirit, and comforting to find that, in spite of disillusions and disappointments, the alternation of exultations and agonies, the soul of the fighting men of England remains unshaken and unconquerable. Three of the Great Powers of Europe espoused the cause of Liberty a year ago; now there are four, and the aid of Italy in engaging and detaching large Austrian forces enables us to contemplate with greater equanimity a month of continuous Russian withdrawal, and the tragic loss of Warsaw and the great fortresses of Novo-

Georgievsk and Brest-Litovsk. And if there is no outward sign of the awakening of Germany, no slackening in frightfulness, no abatement in the blasphemous and overweening confidence of her Ruler and his War-lords who can tell whether they have not moments of self-distrust?

The Wayside Calvary

August 4th 1915.

Now with the full year Memory holds her tryst,
    Heavy with such a tale of bitter loss
As never Earth has suffered since the Christ
       Hung for us on the Cross.

If God, O Kaiser, makes the vision plain;
    Gives you on some lone Calvary to see
The Man of Sorrows Who endured the pain
       and died to set us free—

How will you face beneath its crown of thorn
    That figure stark against the smoking skies,
The arms outstretched, the sacred head forlorn,
       And those reproachful eyes?

How dare confront the false quest with the true,
    Or think what gulfs between the ideals lie
Of Him Who died that men may live—and you
       Who live that man may die?

Ah, turn your eyes away; He reads your heart;
    Pass on and, having done your work abhorred,
Join hands with JUDAS in his place apart,
       You who betrayed your Lord.

It is the way of modern war that we know little of what is going on, least of all on sea. Some of our sailormen have had their chance in the Heligoland Bight, off the Dogger Bank and Falkland Isles, and in the Dardanelles. It is well that we should remember what we owe to the patient vigil of their less fortunate comrades, the officers and men of the Grand Fleet, and to the indefatigable and ubiquitous activities of the ships officially classified as "Light Cruisers (Old)":

AFTER ONE YEAR

From Pole unto Pole, all the oceans between,
Patrolling, protecting, unwearied, unseen,
By night or by noonday, the Navy is there,
And the out-of-date cruisers are doing their share,
The creaky old cruisers whose day is not done,
Built some time before Nineteen-hundred-and-one.

At any rate, we know for certain that British submarines have made their way into the Baltic, a "sea change" extremely disquieting to the Germans, who, for the rest, have suffered in a naval scrap in the Gulf of Riga with the Russians. On the Western front our troops are suffering from two plagues—large shells and little flies. These troubles have not prevented them from scoring a small though costly success at Hooge. From Gallipoli comes the news of fresh deeds of amazing heroism at Suvla Bay and Anzac.

The war of Notes goes on with unabated energy between Germany and the U.S.A. At home a brief period has been set to the pernicious activities of importunate inquisitors by the adjournment of the House till mid-September. "Dr. Punch" is of opinion that the Mother of Parliaments is sorely in need of a rest and needs every hour of a seven weeks' holiday. In the Thrift campaign, which has now set in, everybody expects that everybody else should do his duty; and the universal eruption of posters imploring us to subscribe to the War Loan indicates the emergence of a new Art—that of Government by advertisement. To the obvious appeals to duty, patriotism, conscience, appeals to shame, appeals romantic and even facetious are now added. It may be necessary, but the method is not dignified. All that can be said is that "Govertisement," or government by advertisement, is better than Government by the Press, a new terror with which we are daily threatened.

Mr. Winston Churchill, the greatest of our quick-change political artists, is said to be devoting his leisure to landscape painting. The particular school that he favours is not publicly stated, but we have reason to believe that he intends to be a Leader.

The Archbishop of Cologne says that, on being congratulated on his Eastern successes, the Kaiser "turned his eyes to heaven with the most indescribable expression of intense gratitude and religious fervour." Yes, we can quite imagine that it beggared description. But there is no difficulty in finding the right phrase for his address to the inhabitants of Warsaw: "We wage war only against hostile troops, not against peaceful citizens." It is not *"splendide mendax."* That is the due of boys who overstate, and men who understate, their age in order to serve their country in the field.

A correspondent reminds Mr. Punch that four years ago he wrote as follows: "Lord Haldane, in defending the Territorials, declared that he expects to be dead before any political party seriously suggests compulsory military service. We understand that, since making this statement, our War Minister has received a number of telegrams from Germany wishing him long life." But we suspect that when he said

Officer (to boy of thirteen who, in his effort to get taken on as a bugler, has given his age as sixteen): "Do you know where boys go who tell lies?"
Applicant: "To the Front, sir."

dead he meant politically dead. Still, we owe Lord Haldane the Territorials, and they are doing great work in Europe and most valuable, if thankless, work in India. As "One of the *Punch* brigade" writes: "The hearts of very few of the Territorials now garrisoning India are in their work, though, of course, we know that actually it is essential duty we are performing." "They also serve," who patiently endure the dull routine of existence largely spent in a stifling fort on the blistering and dust-swept plains, and find relief in the smallest incident that breaks the monotony. As, for example, when a quartermaster-sergeant was held up by a native guard at a bridge, and, on demanding an explanation, had his attention directed to the notices on the wall, "Elephants and traction engines are not allowed to cross this bridge."

September, 1915.

The Tsar has succeeded the Grand Nicholas as Generalissimo of his armies, and the great Russian retreat has ended. Yet it would be rash to say that the one event has caused the other. Lord Kitchener's statement that on the Eastern front the Germans had "almost shot their last bolt" is a better summary, and when we reflect on their enormous superiority in artillery and equipment, that is a great tribute to the strategy of the Grand Duke in conducting the most difficult retreat of modern times. Germany, though a mistress of the entire alphabet of frightfulness, is making increasing play with the *U*'s and *Z*'s, and Admiral Percy Scott, who predicted the dangers of the former, is now entrusted with the task of coping with the latter menace.

Five months have elapsed since the sinking of the *Lusitania* and the pro-German campaign in the United States is more active than ever, thanks to the untiring efforts of Count Bernstorff and his worthy ally, Dr. Dumba, in promoting strikes and *sabotage*; but President Wilson, "Le Grand Penseur," declines to be rushed by the interventionists, and is giving his detached consideration to the "concessions" of the German Government in regard to submarine warfare. But three thousand miles of ocean no longer keep America free from strife. The enemy is within her gates, plotting, spying and bribing. The lesser neutrals in Europe find it harder to dissemble their sympathies, but Ferdinand of Bulgaria maintains a vulpine inscrutability.

By way of a sidelight on what happens on the Western front, a wounded officer sends a characteristic account of his experiences after "going over the top" at 3 a.m. "The first remark, as distinct from a shout that I heard after leaving our parapet, came from Private Henry, my most notorious malefactor. As the first attempt at a wire entanglement in our new position went heavenward ten seconds after its emplacement, and a big tree just to our right collapsed suddenly like a dying pig, he turned round with a grin, observing: 'Well, sir, we *do* see a bit of life, if we *don't* make money.' I never saw a man all day who hadn't a grin ready when you passed, and a bit of a *riposte* if you passed the time of day with him." Our officers only think of their men, and the men of their officers. In Gallipoli our soldiers have discovered a new method of annoying the Turk:

We go and bathe, in shameless scores
    Beneath his baleful een,
Disrobe, unscathed, on sacred shores
    And wallow in between;
Nor does a soldier then assume
His university costume,
And though it makes the Faithful fume,
    It makes the Faithless clean.

The return of the wounded to England is marked by strange incidents, pathetic and humorous. Thus it has been reserved for an officer, reported dead in the casualty list, to ring up his people on the telephone and correct "this silly story about my being killed." And the cheerfulness of the limbless men in blue is something wonderful. They "jest at scars," but not because they "never felt a wound." It is a high

The Unsinkable Tirp
German Chancellor: "Well, thank Heaven, that's the last of Tirpitz."
Tirpitz (reappearing): "I don't think!"

privilege to entertain these light-hearted heroes, one of whom recently presented his partner in a lawn tennis match with a fragment of shell taken direct from his "stummick." And the recipient rightly treasures it as a love-token.

Parliament has reassembled, the inquisitors returning (unhappily) like giants refreshed after their holiday. But they sometimes contribute to our amusement, as when one relentless and complacent critic declared that, on the matter of conscription, he should himself "prefer to be guided—very largely—by Lord Kitchener." The concession is something. Most of the importunate questionists are on the other side:

> "Take from us any joys you like," they cry;
>   "We'd bear the loss, however much we missed 'em;
> Let truth and justice, fame and honour die,
>   But spare, o spare, our Voluntary System!"

Amongst other signs of the times the increase of girl gardeners and the sacrifice of flower beds to vegetables are to be noted. But War changes are sometimes disconcerting, even when they are most salutary. For example, there is the *cri de coeur* of a passenger on a Clydebank tramcar in Glasgow on Saturday night, with a lady conductor: "I canna jist bottom this, Tam. It's Seterday nicht an' this is the Clydebank caur, an' there's naebody singin' an' naebody fechtin' wi' the conductor." Liquor control evidently does mean something.

The War vocabulary grows and grows. "Pipsqueaks," "crumps" and "Jack Johnsons," picturesque equivalents for unpleasant things, have long been familiar even to armchair experts. The strangely named "Archie," and "Pacifist," the dismay of scholars—a word "mean as what it's meant to mean"—now come to be added to the list. A new and admirable explanation of the R.F.A., "Ready for anyfink," is attributed to a street Arab. Our children are mostly lapped in blissful ignorance, but their comments are often illuminating. As, for instance, the suggestion of a small child asked to give her idea of a suitable future for Germany and the Kaiser: "After the war I wouldn't let Heligoland belong to anybody. I would put the Germans there, and they should dig and dig and dig until it was all dug into the sea. The Kaiser should be sent to America, and they should be as rude as they liked to him. If he went in a train no one was to offer him a seat; he was to hang on to a strap, and he is to be called Mr. Smith." Cooks are being bribed to stay by the gift of War Bonds. Smart fashionables are flocking to munition works, and some of them sometimes are not unnaturally growing almost frightened at the organising talents they are developing. So are other people.

A vigorous campaign against flies has been initiated by the journal which describes itself as "that paper which gets things done." Nothing is too small for it. Meanwhile it is announced that "Lord Northcliffe is travelling and will be beyond the reach of correspondence until the end of next week." Even he must have an occasional rest from his daily mail.

A HANDY MAN

Marine (somewhat late for parade): "At six o'clock I was a bloomin' 'ousemaid; at seven o'clock I was a bloomin' valet; at eight o'clock I was a bloomin' waiter; an' *now* I'm a bloomin' soldier!"

We have to apologise for any suggestion to the effect that the Huns are devoid of humour. The German Society for the Protection and Preservation of Monuments has held a meeting in Brussels and expressed its thanks to the German Military Authorities for the care they had taken of the Monuments in Belgium. The function ended with an excursion to Louvain, where the delegates, no doubt, enjoyed a happy hour in the Library.

October, 1915.

September ended with the Western front once more ablaze, with bitter fighting at Loos and a great French offensive in Champagne. With October the focus of interest and anxiety shifts to the Balkans. Austrian armies, stiffened with Germans, have again invaded Serbia and again occupied Belgrade. The Allies have landed at Salonika, and Ferdinand of Bulgaria has declared war on Serbia. Thus a new theatre of war has been opened, and though it is well to be rid of a treacherous neutral, the conflict enters on a fresh and formidable phase. When Ferdinand went to Bulgaria he is said to have resolved that if ever there were to be any assassinations he would be on the side of the assassins. He has been true to his word ever since the removal of Stamboloff:

> Here stands the Moslem with his brutal sword
>   Still red and reeking with Armenia's slaughter;
> Here, fresh from Belgium's wastes, the Christian Lord,
>   His heart unsated by the wrong he wrought her;
> And you between them, on your brother's track,
> Sworn, for a bribe, to stick him in the back.

France and England have declared their intention of rendering all possible help to Serbia in her new ordeal, but Greece, false to her treaty with Serbia, and dominated by a pro-German Court and Government, hampers us at every turn. "'Tis Greece, but living Greece no more." So Byron sang, and a Byron *de nos jours* adds a new stanza to his appeal:

> Lo, a new curse—the Teuton bane!
>   Again rings out the trumpet call;
> France, England, Russia, joined again,
>   For freedom fight, for Greece, for all;
> And Greece—shall she that call ignore?
> Then is she living Greece no more!

Life in the trenches grows more strenuous as the output of high explosive increases, and the daily toll of our best and bravest makes grievous reading for the elders at home, "who linger here and droop beneath the heavy burden of our years" though many of them cheerfully undertake the thankless fatigues of guarding the King's highway as specials. But letters from the front still show the same genius for making light of hardship and deadly peril, the same happy gift of extracting amusement from trivial incidents. So those who spend their days and nights under heavy shell fire and heavy rain write to tell you that "tea is the dominating factor of war," or that "the mushrooming and ratting in their latest quarters" are satisfactory. And even the wounded, in comparing the hazards of London with those at the front, only indulge in mild irony at the expense of the "staunch dare-devil souls who stay at home."

In Parliament Sir Edward Carson has explained the reasons of his resignation of office—his difference from his colleagues in the difficulties arising in the Eastern theatre of war; and a resolution has been placed on the order-book proposing the appointment of a Committee of Inquiry on the Dardanelles campaign. No abatement of the plague of questions is yet noticeable, but some slight excuse may be found for the "ragging" of the Censor. This anonymous worthy, it appears, recently excised the words "and the Kings" from the well-known line in Mr. Kipling's "Recessional":

The Captains and the Kings depart.

Apparently the Censor cannot admit any reference to the movements of royalty.

When the Kaiser was at Windsor in 1891 he told the Eton College Volunteers he was glad to see so many of them taking an interest in the study of arms, and hoped that if ever they had to draw their swords in earnest they would use them to some purpose for their country. Now that there are three thousand Etonians at the front he is beginning to be sorry he spoke. The Kaiser, by his own confession, is sorry in another way. He has told a Socialist deputy, "with tears in his eyes," that he was sincerely sorry for France, which was "the greatest disappointment of his life." Even crocodiles sometimes speak the truth unwittingly. Meanwhile the Hamburg *Fremdenblatt* asserts that, "We Germans would gladly follow the Kaiser's lead through the very gates of hell, were it necessary." The qualification is surely superfluous, in the light of the murder of the heroic English hospital matron, Edith Cavell, at Brussels on October 12. Her life was one long act of mercy. She died with unshaken fortitude after the mockery of a trial on a charge of having assisted fugitive British and Belgian prisoners to escape. But her great offence was that she was English. The names of her chief assassins are General Baron von Bissing, the Governor of Brussels, General von Sauberschweig, the Military Governor, and the Baron von der Lancken, the Head of the Political Department. Many years will pass before the echoes of that volley fired at dawn in a Brussels prison yard will die away.

Above:

REALISATION

("When I went to Bulgaria I resolved that if there were to be any assassinations I would be on the side of the assassins." Statement by Ferdinand.)

Opposite:

Landlady: "'Ere's the Zeppelins, sir!"

Lodger: "Right-o! Put 'em down outside."

A new phase has been reached in the Conscription controversy, and the burning question appears to be whether the necessary men are to be compelled to volunteer or persuaded to be compulsorily enrolled. One of our novelist military experts, who is not always lucky with figures, though he thoroughly enjoys them, is alleged to have discovered that there are no more men than can be raised by conscription, but that the same does not, of course, apply to the voluntary system.

The *Daily Mail* asks, "Have we a Foreign Office?" We understand that a search-party is going carefully through Carmelite House. We have certainly got a Chancellor of the Duchy of Lancaster, so efficient in the discharge of his duties that he has made himself an accomplished landscape painter in three months.

A visitor to a remote East Anglian village in search of rest has found recreation in discussing with the inhabitants the Great War, of which he found some of them had heard. "Them there Zett'lins," said one old woman, "I almost shruk as I heerd the mucky varmints a-shovellin' on the coals—dare, dare! How my pore heart did beat!" And an onlooker, who had seen a bomb drop near a church, informed the visitor that it "fared to him like the body of the chach a-floatin' away—that it did and all! It made a clangin' like a covey of lorries with their innards broke loose." Another inhabitant said that he had two boys fighting. "One on 'em is in France, wherever that might be, and Jimmy's in that hare old Dardelles." He couldn't rightly say when the elder had gone out, "but it might be a yare ago come muck-spreadin'."

November, 1915.

More money and more men is still the cry. The war is now costing five millions a day, and the new vote of credit for £400,000,000 will only carry us on till the middle of February. This is "Derby's Day," and the new Director of Recruiting inspires confidence in his ability to make good, in spite of the Jeremiads of Lord Courtney and Lord Loreburn. The lot of a Coalition Government is never easy, and public opinion clamours not for Jeremiahs but for Jonahs to lighten the Ship of State. Mr. Winston Churchill, wearying of his sinecure at the Duchy of Lancaster, has resigned office, explained himself in a long speech, and rejoined his regiment at the Western front. Lord Fisher, whose doubts and hesitations about the Dardanelles expedition were referred to by the late First Lord, has been content to leave his record of sixty-one years' service in the hands of his countrymen. In the briefest maiden speech ever delivered in either House he stated that it was "unfitting to make personal explanations affecting the national interest when my country is in the midst of a great war." Here at least the traditions of the "Silent Service" have been worthily maintained, just as they are maintained by the Port Officer R.N.R. at an Oriental seaport, a thousand miles from the front, out of the limelight, with no chance of glory, with fever from morn till night, who "worries along by the grace of God and the blessing of cheap cheroots."

In Flanders the rain has begun its winter session, and, as a military humorist put it, trench warfare is becoming a constant drain. The problem of parapet mending has been reduced to arithmetical form à la Colenso, as follows: "If two inches of rain per diem brings down one quarter of a company's parapet, and one company, working about twenty-six hours per diem, can revet one-eighth of a company's parapet, how long will your trenches last—given the additional premises that no revetments to speak of are to be had, and that two inches of rain is only a minimum ration?" The infantryman finds the men of the R.F.C. interesting and stimulating companions. "These airy fellows talk of war as if it were a day's shooting, and they the cock pheasants with the best of the fun up aloft. Upon my word, the hen who hatched such birds should be a proud, if anxious, mother." The same correspondent sends a pleasant account of the mutual estimates of French and English, prompted by their experiences as brothers in arms. "Our idea of our Ally as a soldier is that his *élan* and gay courage are very much more remarkable even than supposed; but for the dull, heavy work of continued warfare there is wanted, if we may say so without offence, the more stolid qualities of the English. On the other hand, the French opinion of their Ally as a soldier is that his dash and devilment are really astonishing, even to the most expectant critic; but for the sordid, monotonous strain of this trench business it needs (a thousand pardons!) the duller persistence of the French."

In Greece the quick change of Premiers proceeds with kaleidoscopic rapidity. The attitude of the successive Prime Ministers has been described as (1) Tender and affectionate neutrality toward the Entente Powers; (2) Malevolent impartiality toward

THE PERSUADING OF TINO

Paddy (who has had his periscope smashed by a bullet): "Sure there's seven years' bad luck for the poor devil that broke that, anyhow."

the Central Powers; (3) Inert cupidity toward all the belligerent Powers; (4) Genial inability; (5) Strict pusillanimity.

Lord Milner has gone so far in the House of Lords as to say that "such war news as is published has from first to last been seriously misleading." The Balkan intelligence that is allowed to reach us does not exactly deserve this censure. To call it misleading would be too high praise; it seldom rises beyond a level of blameless irrelevance. It is hardly a burlesque of the facts to say that a cable from Amsterdam informs us that the Copenhagen correspondent of the *Echo de Paris* learns from Salonika, *via* Lemnos and Nijni Novgorod, that in high official circles in Bukarest it is rumoured that in Constantinople the situation is considered grave; and then we are warned that too much credence must not be given to this report. The number of Censors at the Press Bureau being exactly forty, and their minute knowledge of English literature having been displayed on several occasions, it is said that Sir John Simon contemplates their incorporation as an Academy of "Immortals—for the duration of the War."

Mr. Punch's correspondent "Blanche" sends distressing details of some of the new complaints contracted by smart war workers. These include munition-wrists, shell-makers' crouch, neuro-committee-itis, and Zeppelin-eye through looking up into the sky too long with a telescope.

A great deal depends on what you look at and what you look through. Thus Mr. Walter Long says that when he reads carping criticisms upon the conduct of the War he looks through his window at the people in the street and is always surprised to see the quiet steadfast manner in which they are going about their business. It is a good plan, but not always successful. The Kaiser got his view of the Irish people through a Casement, and it was entirely erroneous.

The *Cologne Gazette* has stated that "there is in England no real soldiers' humour such as we have." Certainly we have nothing like it, though we confess to preferring the home grown brand.

December, 1915.

Kut and Ctesiphon, Ctesiphon and Kut. Thus may the events of the last month in Mesopotamia, no longer a "blessed word," be expressed in a bald formula, which takes no account of the unavailing heroism of General Townshend's small but splendid force. Things have not been going well in the East. The Allies have been unable to save Serbia, Monastir has fallen, and our lines have been withdrawn to Salonika. The experts are now divided into two camps, the Westerners and the Easterners, and the former, pointing to the evacuation of Gallipoli, are loud in their denunciations of costly "side-shows," and the folly of strengthening Germany's hold on Turkey by killing out the Turks, instead of concentrating all our forces on killing the Germans on the Western front. The time is not yet come to decide which is right. But all are agreed with the British officer who described the Australian soldier at Gallipoli as "the bravest thing God ever made," and so prompted these lines:

Bravest, where half a world of men
    Are brave beyond all earth's rewards,
So stoutly none shall charge again
    Till the last breaking of the swords;
Wounded or hale, won home from war,
    Or yonder by the Lone Pine laid;
Give him his due for evermore—
    "The bravest thing God ever made!"

Though the wings of the angel of Peace cannot be heard, peace kite-flying has already begun in Vienna, but Germany is anxious to represent it as unauthorised and improper. Mr. Henry Ford's voyage to Europe on the *Oscar II* with a strangely assorted group of Pacificists does more credit to his heart than his head, and the conflicting elements in his party have earned for his ship the name of "The Tug of Peace." Anyhow, England is taking no risks on the strength of these irregular "overtures." A vote has been passed for a further increase of our "contemptible little Army" to four millions; and the manufacture of high explosive goes on in an ever-increasing ratio. Sir Douglas Haig has succeeded Sir John French as Commander-in-Chief of our Armies in France; Sir William Robertson is the new Chief of Staff—Scotsmen both of the finest type—and the appointments are universally approved, even by the *Daily Mail*. The temper of the men in France is well hit off by an officer when he says that "Atkins is really best when an ordinary mortal might be contemplating suicide or desertion." And officers arriving on leave at Victoria at 2 a.m. are driven to the conclusion that they are sent back to England from time to time to check their optimism, which at the front survives even being sent to so-called rest camps in the middle of a malodorous marsh for nine hours' military training *per diem*. The "philosophy of Thomas" is inscrutable, but no doubt he derives satisfaction from comparisons:

If we're standin' in two foot o' water, you see
Quite likely the Boches are standin' in three;
An' though the keen frost may be ticklin' our toes,
'Oo doubts that the Boches' 'ole bodies is froze?

So 'ere's our philosophy, simple an' plain:
Wotever we 'ates in the bloomin' campaign,
'Tis balm to our souls, as we grumble an' cuss,
To feel that the Boches are 'atin' it wuss.

AN UNAUTHORISED FLIRTATION
The Kaiser (to Austrian Emperor): "Franz! Franz! I'm surprised and pained."

Tommy (finding a German prisoner who speaks English): "Look what you done to me, you blighters! 'Ere—'ave a cigarette?"

Hardest of all is the lot of the trooper in the trenches, who "thinks all day and dreams all night of a slap-bang, tally-ho! open fight," but for the time being "like a blinded mole toils in a furrow and lives in a hole."

The National Thrift campaign is carried on with great earnestness in Parliament. Luxury, waste, unnecessary banquets, high legal salaries have all come under the lash of the economy hunters. Of the maxim that "Charity begins at home," they have, however, so far shown no appreciation beyond abstaining from voting any addition to their salary of £400 a year. Mr. Asquith's announcement that he takes his salary, and is going to continue taking it, has naturally lifted a great weight from the minds of these vicarious champions of economy.

Evidence of the chastened condition of the enemy is to be found in the statement on the official notepaper of Wolff's Telegraphic Bureau "that it assumes no responsibility of any kind for the accuracy of the news which it circulates." But there is no confirmation of the report that its dispatches will in future be known as "Lamb's Tales." The German Imperial Chancellor has replied to an appeal from a deputation of German Roman Catholics on behalf of the Armenians that "The German Government, in friendly communication with the Turkish Government, has been at constant pains to better the situation of Turkey's Christian subjects." Thanks to this friendly intervention, more than half a million Armenians will never suffer again from Turkish misrule.

Mr. Roosevelt has added to the picturesqueness of political invective by describing Mr. Wilson's last Presidential message as "worthy of a Byzantine logothete." It is not often that one finds a rough-rider and ex-cowboy who is able to tackle a don in his own lingo. But Tommy at the front manages to converse with the *poilu* without any vocabulary at all:

I met a chap the other day a-roostin' in a trench,
'E didn't know a word of ours nor me a word of French,
An' 'ow it was we managed—well, I cannot understand,
But I never used the phrase-book, though I 'ad it in my hand.

I winked at 'im to start with; 'e grinned from ear to ear;
An' 'e says "Tipperary," an' I says "Sooveneer";
'E 'ad my only Woodbine, I 'ad 'is thin cigar,
Which set the ball a-rollin', an' so—well, there you are!

I showed 'im next my wife an' kids, 'e up an' showed me 'is,
Them funny little Frenchy kids with 'air all in a frizz;
"Annette," 'e says, "Louise," 'e says, an' 'is tears began to fall;
We was comrades when we parted, but we'd 'ardly spoke at all.

January, 1916.

The New Year brings us a mixed bag of tricks, good and bad. Our armies grow in numbers and efficiency, in men and munitions. The new Commander-in-Chief on the Western front, and his new Chief of Staff, inspire confidence in all ranks, combatant and non-combatant. John Ward, the Labour Member, hitherto a strong opponent of conscription, and now a full-blown Colonel, has hurried over from the front to defend the Compulsory Service Bill in a manly and animated speech, and the Bill, despite the "Pringling" and pacificism of a small but local minority, has passed through Committee.

Against these encouraging omens we have to set the complete evacuation of Gallipoli, the scene of unparalleled heroism and unavailing sacrifice, the fall of Monastir, the overrunning of Serbia, labour troubles on the Clyde, and the ignominious exemption of Ireland from the Military Service Bill. General Townshend, *rebus angustis animosus*—"in a tight place but full of beans"—is besieged in Kut, and the relieving forces have not been able to dislodge the Turks. Climate and weather and *terrain* are all against us.

Humanitarian Pacificists are much impressed by Germany's piteous lamentations over the brutality of the blockade. In these appeals to America optimists detect signs

FOR NEUTRALS
"Why do we torpedo passenger ships?
Because we are being starved by the infamous
English."

FOR NATIVES
"Who says we are in distress?
Look what our splendid organisation
is doing."

of cracking. Cooler observers explain them as evidence of her policy of shamming
dead.

English mothers who have lost their only sons cannot be expected to show sympathy for an Emperor who combines the professions of a Jekyll with the ferocity of
a Hyde. Yet few of them would rewrite the record of these short lives; their pride is
greater than their pain.

While the daily toll of life is heavy, War, shorn of its pomp and pageantry, drags
wearily in the trenches. The Lovelace of to-day is a troglodyte, biding his time
patiently, but often a prey to *ennui*. This is how he writes to Lucasta to correct the
portrait painted by her fancy:

Above, the sky is very grey, the world is very damp.
His light the sun denies by day, the moon by night her lamp;
Across the landscape, soaked and sad, the dull guns answer back,
And through the twilight's futile hush spasmodic rifles crack.

The papers haven't come to-day to show how England feels;
The hours go lame and languidly between our Spartan meals;
We've written letters till we're tired, with not a thing to tell
Except that nothing's doing, weather beastly, writer well.

So when you feel for us out here—as well I know you will—
Then sympathise with thousands for their country sitting still;
Don't picture battle-pieces by the lurid Press adored,
But miles and miles of Britishers, in burrows, badly bored.

Small wonder that Lovelace in the trenches envies the Flying Man:

He rides aloof on god-like wings,
    Taking no thought of wire or mud,
Saps, smells, or bugs—the mundane things
    That sour our lives and have our blood.

The roads we trudged with feet of lead,
    The shadows of his pinions skim;
The river where we piled our dead
    Is but a silver thread to him.

Lovelace in the air might tell another story; but both are at one with their proto-type in the spirit which made him say: "I could not love thee, dear, so much, loved I not honour more," though neither of them would say it.

In this context one may add that the Flying Men are not alone in exciting envy. Bread is the staff of life, and in the view of certain officers in the trenches the life of the Staff is one long loaf.

The discussion on the withdrawal of Members' salaries has died down. The incident is now buried, and here is its epitaph:

Some three-score years or so ago six hundred gallant men
Made a charge that cost old England dear; they lost four hundred then:
To-day six hundred make a charge that costs the country dear,
But now they take four hundred each—four hundred pounds a year.

Our journalists have been visiting the Fleet, and one of them, in a burst of can-dour tempered with caution, declares that "one would like to describe much more than one has seen, but that is impossible." Some other correspondents have found no such difficulty. But for admirable candour commend us to the *Daily Mail* of December 24, where we read, "The *Daily Mail* will not be published to-morrow, and for that reason we seize the occasion to-day of bidding our readers a Merry Christmas"—and a very good reason too. Mr. Punch is glad to reprint a ten-year-old girl's essay on "Patriotism": "Patriotism is composed of patriots, and they are people who live in Ireland and want Mr. Redmond or other people to be King of Ireland. They are very brave, some of them, and are so called after St. Patrick, who is Ireland's

Tommy (dictating letter to be sent to his wife):
"The nurses here are a very plain lot—"
Nurse: "Oh, come! I say! That's not very polite to us."
Tommy: "Never mind, Nurse, put it down. It'll please her!"

private saint. The patriots who are brave make splendid soldiers. The patriots who are not brave go to America." And here is a topical extract from a letter written to a loved one from the Front:

> "I received your dear little note in a sandbag. You say that you hope the sandbag stops a bullet. Well, to tell the truth, I hope it don't, as I have been patching my trousers with it."

Tommy is adding to his other great qualities that of diplomacy, to judge from the incident illustrated above.

February, 1916.

The Epic of the Dardanelles is closed; that of Verdun has begun, and all eyes are focused on the tremendous struggle for the famous fortress. The Crown Prince has still his laurels to win, and it is clear that no sacrifice of German "cannon fodder" will be too great to deter him from pushing the stroke home. Fort Douaumont has fallen, and the hill of the Mort Homme has already terribly justified its cadaverous name. The War-lords of Germany are sorely in need of a spectacular success even though they purchase it at a great price, for they are very far from having everything their own way. Another Colony has gone the way of Tsing-tau, New Guinea and South-West Africa. The German Kamerun has cried "Kamerad!" General Smuts, like Botha, "Boer and Briton too," has gone off to take command in East Africa, and in the Caucasus Erzerum has fallen to the Russians. The Kaiser is reported to be bitterly disappointed with Allah.

Sir Edward Grey is not altogether satisfied with the conduct of the Neutral Powers. He has no desire to make things as irksome to them as some of his critics desire. But he has pointed out that in the matter of preventing supplies from reaching the enemy by circuitous routes Great Britain has her own work to do, and means to do it thoroughly.

The miraculous forbearance of President Wilson, in face of the activities of Count Bernstorff, is even more trying to a good many of his countrymen than it is to the belligerent Briton. Mr. Roosevelt, for instance, derives no satisfaction from being the fellow-countryman of a man who can "knock spots" off Job for patience. The *New York Life* has long criticised the President with a freedom far eclipsing anything in the British Press. It has now crowned its "interventionist" campaign by a "John Bull number," the most generous and graceful tribute ever paid to England by the American Press.

The Military Service Bill has passed through both Houses, and may be trusted to hasten still further the amazing growth of our once "contemptible little" Army.

Above:

THE CHALLENGE

"Halt! Who comes there?" "Neutral." "Prove it!"

"What I would say to Neutrals is this: Do they admit our right to apply the principles which were applied by the American Government in the war between North and South—to apply those principles to modern conditions and to do our best to prevent trade with the enemy through neutral countries? If the answer is that we are not entitled to do that, then I must say definitely it is a departure from neutrality."—Sir Edward Grey

Opposite:

Grannie (dragged out of bed at 1.30 a.m., and being hurriedly dressed as the bombs begin to fall): "Nancy, these stockings are not a pair."

The pleasantest incident during the month at Westminster has been the tribute paid to the gallantry and self-sacrifice of the officers and men of our mercantile marine. The least satisfactory aspect of Parliamentary activity has been the ventilation of silly rumours at Question time, in which Mr. Ginnell has been so well to the fore as to suggest some subtle connection between cattle-driving and hunting for mares' nests.

Steps have already been taken to restrict the imports of luxuries; and Ministers are believed to be unanimous in regarding "ginger" as an article whose importation might be profitably curtailed. It has been calculated that the annual expenses saved by the closing of the London Museums and Galleries amount to about one-fifth of the public money spent on the salaries of Members of Parliament. In other words:

Let Art and Science die,
But give us still our old Loquacity.

Intellectual retrenchment, of course, is desirable,

But let us still keep open one collection
    Of curiosities and quaint antiques,
Under immediate Cabinet direction—
    The finest specimens of talking freaks,

First Lady: "That's one of them Australian soldiers."
Second Lady: "How do you know?'
First Lady: "Why, can't you see the kangaroo feathers in his hat?"

Who constitute our most superb museum,
Judged by the salaries with which we fee 'em.

Lord Sumner, however, seems to have no illusions on this score. He is reported to have said that "if the House of Lords and the House of Commons could be taken and thrown into a volcano every day the loss represented would be less than the daily loss of the campaign." It sounds a drastic remedy, but might be worth trying.

Field-Marshal Lord French has taken over the responsibility for home defence against enemy aircraft, with Sir Percy Scott as his expert adviser. But the status of Sir Percy, who, as officially announced, "has not quite left the Admiralty and has not quite joined the War Office," seems to suggest "a kind of giddy harumfrodite—soldier an' sailor too."

The War fosters the study of natural and unnatural history. Many early nestings are recorded as the result of mild weather, and at least one occasional visitor (*Polonius bombifer*) has laid eggs in various parts of the country.

March, 1916.

The month of the War god has again justified its name and its traditions. Both entry and exit have been leonine. The new submarine "frightfulness" began on the 1st, and the battle round Verdun, in which the fate of Paris, to say the least, is involved, has raged with unabated fury throughout the entire month.

Germany's junior partners, Turkey and Bulgaria, are for the moment more concerned with bleeding Germany than with shedding their blood for her; Enver Pasha is reported to have gone to pay a visit to the tomb of the Prophet at Medina; Portugal, our oldest ally, is now officially at war with Germany, and the dogs of frightfulness are already toasting "*der Tagus.*"

On our share of the Western front there is still what is nominally described as a "lull." But, as a young officer writes, "you must not imagine that life here is all honey. Even here we do a bit for our eight-and-sixpence." Once upon a time billets were billets. They now very often admit of being shelled with equal exactitude from due in front and due in rear, and water is laid on throughout. "It is a fact well known to all our most widely circulated photographic dailies that the German gunners waste a power of ammunition. The only criticism I have to make is that I wish they would waste it more carefully. The way they go strewing the stuff about around us is such that they're bound to hit someone or something before long. Still, we have only two more days in these trenches, and they seldom give us more than ten thousand shells a day."

Letters from second-lieutenants seldom go beyond a gentle reminder that their life is not an Elysium. They offer a strange contrast to the activities of Parliamentary grousers and scapegoat hunters. If the Germans were in occupation of the Black Country, if Oxford were being daily shelled as Rheims is, and if with a favouring breeze London could hear the dull rumble of the bombardment as Paris can, one wonders if Members would still be encumbering the Order-paper with the vexatious trivialities that now find place there, or emitting what a patriotic Labour Member picturesquely described as "the croakings and bleatings of the fatted lambs who have besmirched their country." *Per contra* we welcome the optimism of Mr. Asquith in discussing new Votes of Credit, though he reminds us of Micawber calculating his indebtedness for the benefit of Traddles. It will be remembered that when the famous IOU had been handed over, Copperfield remarked, "I am persuaded not only that this was quite the same to Mr. Micawber as paying the money, but that Traddles himself hardly knew the difference until he had had time to think about it." Then we have had the surprising but welcome experience of Mr. Tim Healy championing the Government against Sir John Simon's attack on the Military Service Bill; and have listened to Lord Montagu of Beaulieu's urgent plea in the Lords for unity of air control, a proposal which Lord Haldane declared could not be adopted without some "violent thinking." Most remarkable of all has been Mr.

Above:
TO THE GLORY OF FRANCE
Verdun, February—March, 1916

Opposite:
MULE HUMOUR

"He's kicked the Corporal!"

"He's kicked the Vet.!!"

"He's kicked the Transport Officer!!!"

"He's kicked the Colonel!!!!"

Churchill's intervention in the debate on the Naval Estimates, his gloomy review of the situation—Mr. Churchill is always a pessimist when out of office—and the marvellous magnanimity of his suggestion that Lord Fisher should be reinstated at the Admiralty, on the ground that his former antagonist was the only possible First Sea Lord. Mr. Balfour dealt so faithfully with these criticisms and suggestions that there seems to be no truth in the report that Mr. Churchill has been asked to join the Government as Minister of Admonitions. A new and coruscating star has swum into our Parliamentary ken in the shape of the Member for Mid-Herts, and astronomers have labelled it "Pegasus π β." When the House of Commons passed the Bill prohibiting duels it ought to have made an exception in favour of its own Members. Nothing would have done more to raise the tone of debate, for offenders against decorum would gradually have eliminated one another. Yet Parliament has its merits, not the least of them being the scope it still affords for hereditary talent. Lord Derby, at the moment the most prominent man on the Home Front after the Premier, is the grandson of the "Rupert of Debate," and the new Minister of Blockade enters on his duties close on fifty years after another Lord Robert Cecil entered the Cabinet of Lord Derby. So history repeats itself with a difference. In spite of the Coalition, or perhaps because of it, the old strife of Whigs and Tories has revived, though the lines of cleavage are quite different from what they were. Thus the new Tories are the men who believe that the War is going to be decided by battles in Flanders and the North Sea, and would sacrifice everything for victory, even the privilege of abusing the Government. The new Whigs are the men who consider that the House of Commons is the decisive arena, and that even the defeat of the Germans would be dearly purchased at the cost of the individual's right to say and do what he pleased.

After the exhibition of Mr. Augustus John's portrait of Mr. Lloyd George, the most startling personal event of the month has been the dismissal of Grand Admiral Tirpitz. According to one account, he resigned because he could not take the German Fleet out. According to another, it was because he could no longer take the German people in.

At Oxford the Hebdomadal Council have suspended the filling of the Professorship of Modern Greek for six months. Apparently there is no one about just now who understands the modern Greek. A French correspondent puts it somewhat differently: "*La Grèce Antique:* Hellas. *La Grèce Moderne:* Hélas!"

April, 1916.

Who would have thought when the month opened that at its close a new front within the Four Seas would be added to our far-flung line, Dublin's finest street half ruined, Ireland placed under martial law? Certainly not Mr. Birrell or Mr. Redmond

The Vicar: "These Salonikans, Mrs. Stubbs, are, of course, the Thessalonians to whom St. Paul wrote his celebrated letters."
Mrs. Stubbs: "Well, I 'ope 'e'd better luck with 'is than I 'ave. I sent my boy out there three letters and two parcels, and I ain't got no answer to 'em yet."

or the Irish Nationalist Members. The staunchest Unionist would acquit Mr. William O'Brien of any menace when in the Budget Debate, three weeks before the Rebellion of Easter Week, he gave it as his opinion that Ireland ought to be omitted from the Budget altogether. So, too, with Mr. Tim Healy, whose principal complaint was that the tax on railway tickets would put a premium on foreign travel; that people would go to Paris instead of Dublin, and Switzerland instead of Killarney. No, so far as the Government and Ireland's Parliamentary representatives went, it was a bolt from the blue—or the green. Mr. Birrell, Chief Secretary for Ireland for nine years, a longer period than any of his predecessors, has shown himself conspicuous at once by his absence and his innocence, and England in her hour of need, with the submarine peril daily growing and Kut starved out after a heroic defence, stands to pay dearly for the privilege of entrusting the administration of Ireland to an absentee humorist.

On the Western front Verdun still rivets all eyes. The German hordes are closing in on the fortress, but at a heavier cost for each mile gained than they have ever paid before.

Germany's colossal effort would inspire admiration as well as respect if she would only fight clean. The ugly stories of her treatment of prisoners have now culminated in the terrible record of the typhus-stricken camp at Wittenberg, where the German doctors deserted their post.

THE REPUDIATION

Martin Luther (to Shakespeare): "I see my countrymen claim you as one of them. You may thank God that you're not that. They have made my Wittenberg—ay, and all Germany—to stink in my nostrils."

The report of Mr. Justice Younger's Committee, in which the tale of this atrocity is fully told, is being circulated in neutral countries, and Mr. Will Thorne has suggested that it should also be sent to our conscientious objectors. It is well to administer some sort of corrective to the information diffused by the neutral newsmonger:

Who cheers us when we're in the blues,
With reassuring German news,
Of starving Berliners in queues?
    The Neutral.

And then, soon after, tells us they
Are feeding nicely all the day,
And in the old familiar way?
    The Neutral.

Who sees the Kaiser in Berlin,
Dejected, haggard, old as sin,
And shaking in his hoary skin?
    The Neutral.

Then says he's quite a Sunny Jim,
That buoyant health and youthful vim
Are sticking out all over him?
    The Neutral.

Who tells us tales of Krupp's new guns,
Much larger than the other ones,
And endless trains chock-full of Huns?
    The Neutral.

And then, when our last hope has fled,
Declares the Huns are either dead
Or hopelessly dispirited?
    The Neutral.

In short, who seems to be a blend
Of Balaam's Ass, the bore's godsend,
And *Mrs. Gamp's* elusive friend?
    The Neutral.

In Parliament we have had the biggest Budget ever known introduced in the shortest Budget speech of the last half-century, at any rate. Mr. Pemberton Billing is doing his best every Tuesday to bring the atmosphere of the aerodrome into the House. Mr. Tennant has promised his sympathetic consideration to Mr. Billing's offer personally to organise raids on the enemy's aircraft bases, and the House is bearing up as well as can be expected under the shadow of this impending bereave-

THE GRAPES OF VERDUN
The Old Fox: "You don't seem to be getting much nearer them?"
The Cub: "No, Father. Hadn't we better give it out that they're sour?"

ment. Mr. Swift MacNeill is busy with his patriotic effort to purge the roll of the
Lords of the peerages now held by enemy dukes. For the rest, up to Easter Week, the
Parliamentary situation has been described as "a cabal every afternoon and a crisis
every second day."

Visitor (at Private Hospital): "Can I see Lieutenant Barker, please?"
Matron: "We do not allow ordinary visiting. May I ask if you are a relative?"
Visitor (boldly): "Oh, yes! I'm his sister."
Matron: "Dear me! I'm very glad to meet you. *I'm his mother.*"

It is one of the strange outcomes of this wonderful time that there is more gaiety as well as more suffering in hospitals during the War than in peace. Certainly such a request would never have been heard in normal years as that recently made by a nurse to a roomful of irrepressible Tommies at a private hospital:

"A message has just come in to ask if the hospital will make a little less noise as the lady next door has a touch of headache."

For shouting "The Zepps are coming!" a Grimsby girl has been fined £1. It was urged in defence that the girl suffered from hallucinations, one being that she was a daily newspaper proprietor. But the recent Zeppelin raids have not been without their advantages. In a spirit of emulation an ambitious hen at Acton has laid an egg weighing 5¼ oz.

May, 1916.

Verdun still holds out: that is the best news of the month. The French with inexorable logic continue to exact the highest price for the smallest gain of ground. If the Germans are ready to give 100,000 men for a hill or part of a hill they may have it. If they will give a million men they may perhaps have Verdun itself. But so far their Pyrrhic victories have stopped short of this limit, and Verdun, like Ypres, battered, ruined and evacuated by civilians, remains a symbol of Allied tenacity and the will to resist.

The months in war-time sometimes belie their traditions, but it is fitting that in May we should have enlisted a new Ally— the Sun. The Daylight Saving Bill became Law on May 17. Here is a true economy, and our only regret is that Mr. Willett, the chief promoter of a scheme complacently discussed during his lifetime as ingenious but impracticable, should not have lived to witness its swift and unmurmuring acceptance under stress of war.

The official *communiqués* from the Irish Front in the earlier stages of the Dublin rebellion did not long maintain their roseate complexion. Even before the end of April a Secret Session—the second in a week—was held to discuss the Irish situation. By a strange coincidence this Secret Session immediately followed the grant by the Commons of a Return relating to Irish Lunacy accounts. From the meagre official summary we gather that the absence of reporters has at least the negative advantage of shortening speeches. In a very few days, however, the Prime Minister discarded reticence, admitting the gravity of the situation, the prevalence of street fighting, the spread of the insurrection in the West, the appointment of Sir John Maxwell to the supreme command, and the placing of the Irish Government under his orders. The inevitable sequel—the execution of the responsible insurrectionist leaders—has led to vehement protests from Messrs. Dillon and O'Brien against

HELD!

militarist brutality. The House of Commons is a strange place. When Mr. Birrell rose on May 3 to give an account of his nine years' stewardship, the Unionists, and not the Unionists alone, were thinking of a lamp-post in Whitehall. When he had concluded his pathetic apologia and confessed his failure to estimate accurately the strength of Sinn Fein, members were almost ready to fall on his neck, but they no longer wanted his head. Even Sir Edward Carson admitted that Mr. Birrell had been well intentioned and had done his best. By the middle of the month Mr. Asquith had gone to Ireland, in the hope of discovering some arrangement for the future which would commend itself to all parties. By the 25th he was back in his place after nine days in Dublin. But he had no panacea of his own to prescribe; no cut-and-dried plan for the regeneration of Ireland. All he could say was that Mr. Lloyd George had been deputed by the Cabinet to confer with the various Irish leaders, and the choice is generally approved. If anyone knows how to handle high explosives without causing a premature concussion it should be the Minister of Munitions.

Ireland has dominated the political scene at home, for it is impossible not to connect our new commitments across St. George's Channel with the introduction and passing of the new Military Service Bill establishing compulsion for all men, married or single—always excepting Ireland. The question of man-power is paramount. Mr. Asquith is at last convinced that "Wait and See" must yield to "Do it Now": that the nation won't have the sword of Damocles hanging over its head any longer, but

WANTED—A ST. PATRICK
Sr. Augustine Birrell: "I'm afraid I'm not so smart as my brother-saint at dealing with this kind of thing. I'm apt to take reptiles too lightly."

will have compulsion in its hand at once. On the progress of the War Mr. Asquith has said little in Open Session, but any omission on his part has been made good by Mr. Churchill, now home on unlimited leave, who has spoken at great length on the proper use of armies.

Mr. Arthur Ponsonby and Mr. Ramsay MacDonald, who raised the question of Peace on Empire Day, urging the Government to open negotiations with Germany, have elicited from the Foreign Secretary the deliberate statement that the only terms of peace which the German Government had ever put forward were the terms of victory for Germany, and that we could not reason with the German people so long as they were fed with lies.

Mr. Henry James, who so nobly repaid the hospitality England was proud to show him by adopting her nationality in her hour of greatest need, said shortly before his death that nothing grieved him more than the constant loss of England's "best blood, seed and breed." The mothers of England "give their sons," but they know that the choice did not rest with them:

We did not give you—all unasked you went,
    Sons of a greater motherhood than ours;

To our proud hearts your young brief lives were lent,
    Then swept beyond us by resistless powers.
Only we hear, when we have lost our all,
       That far clear call.

But how can the grief be measured of those

          Whose best,
    Eager to serve a higher quest
And in the Great Cause know the joy of battle,
    Gallant and young, by traitor hands,
    Leagued with a foe from alien lands,
Struck down in cold blood, fell like butchered cattle?

Though Ireland is not for the moment a source of humour she contrives to be the cause of it in others. A daily paper tells us that Sir Robert Chalmers is to be "Permanent Under Secretary of Ireland *pro tem.*" Another daily paper, the *Daily Mail*, to be precise, has discovered a new test of valour: "Mr. Mellish, a regular reader of the *Daily Mail* for years, was awarded the V.C. last month for conspicuous bravery."

June, 1916.

At last the long vigil in the North Sea has ended in the glorious if indecisive battle of Jutland, the greatest sea fight since Trafalgar. Yet was it indecisive? After the momentary dismay caused by the first Admiralty *communiqué* with its over-estimate of our losses, public confidence, shaken where it was strongest, has been restored by further information and by the admissions of the enemy. We have to mourn the loss of many ships, still more the loss of splendid ships' companies and their heroic captains. We can sympathise with the cruel disappointment of those who, after bearing the brunt of the action, were robbed of the opportunity of overwhelming their enemy by failing light and the exigencies of a strategy governed in the last resort by political caution. But look at the sequel. The German Fleet, badly battered, retires to port; and despite the pæans of exultation from their Admirals, Kaiser, and Imperial Chancellor, remains there throughout the month. Will it ever come out again? Meanwhile, Wilhelmshaven is closed indefinitely, and nobody is allowed to see those sheep in Wolff's clothing—the "victorious fleet." The true verdict, so far as we can judge, may be expressed in homely phrase: The British Navy has taken a knock but given a harder one. We can stand it and they can't.

Within a week of Jutland the Empire has been stirred to its depths by the tragic death of Lord Kitchener in the *Hampshire*, blown up by a mine off the Shetlands on her voyage to Archangel. On the eve of starting on his mission to Russia his last official act had been to meet his critics of the House of Commons face to face, reply to their questions and leave them silenced and admiring. On the day of the battle of Jutland these critics had moved the Prime Minister to declare that Lord Kitchener was personally entitled to the credit for the amazing expansion of the army. Sir Mark Sykes, no mean authority, asserted that in Germany our War Secretary was feared as a great organiser, while in the East his name was one to conjure with; and Sir George Reid, a worthy representative of the Dominions, observed that his chief fault was that he was "not clever at circulating the cheap coin of calculated civilities which enable inferior men to rise to positions to which they are not entitled." These tributes were delivered in his lifetime; they deserve to be contrasted with the appreciations of those journalists who clamoured for his appointment, then clamoured for his dismissal, and profaned his passing with their insincere eulogies. Three weeks of Recess elapsed before the Houses could render homage to the illustrious dead. In the Lords the debt has been paid by a statesman, Lord Lansdowne, a soldier, Lord French, and a friend, Lord Derby. In the Commons the speeches were all touched with genuine emotion and the sense of personal loss. Through all these various tributes rang the note of duty well done, and Mr. Bonar Law did well to remind the House of the sure instinct which caused Lord Kitchener to realise at the very outset the gigantic nature of the present War. In a sense his loss is irreparable, yet his great work was accomplished before he died. Sometimes accused of expecting others to achieve the impossible, he had achieved it himself in the crowning miracle of his life, the improvisation of the New Armies.

The violation of Greek territory by the Bulgarian troops, as might be expected, has not led to any effective protest from King Constantine. On the contrary, one seems to hear this benevolent neutral deprecating any apology on the part of King Ferdinand: "Please make yourself at home. This is Liberty Hall."

It is otherwise with the irruption of the Russians under General Brusiloff. His great offensive is a source of offence to the Austrians, who have good reason to complain that the "steam-roller" is exceeding the speed limit. Or to change the metaphor, the bear and his tormentor have changed places.

Ireland has receded a little from her place in the limelight, and though debates on martial law continue, and Irish members ask an inordinate number of questions arising out of the hot Easter week in Dublin, the temperature is no longer "'98 in the shade" as a local wit described it at the time. Ministers are extremely economical of information: the anticipated settlement still hangs fire, and there are increasing fears that it will not hold water.

A number of professional fortune-tellers have been fined at Southend for having predicted Zeppelins. The fraudulent nature of their pretensions was sufficiently

THE LOST CHIEF
In Memory of Field-Marshal Earl Kitchener, Maker of Armies

manifest, since even the authorities had been unable to foresee the Zeppelins until some time after they had arrived.

The discussions in Parliament and out of it of the way in which things get into the papers which oughtn't to, are dying down. A daily paper, however, has revived them by the head line, "Cabinet leekage." Now, why, in wonder, do they spell it in that way?

THE FAR-REACHING EFFECT OF THE RUSSIAN PUSH

It is quite impossible to keep pace with all the new incarnations of women in war-time—'bus-conductress, ticket-collector, lift-girl, club waitress, post-woman, bank clerk, motor-driver, farm-labourer, guide, munition maker. There is nothing new in the function of ministering angel: the myriad nurses in hospital here or abroad are only carrying out, though in greater numbers than ever before, what has always been woman's mission. But whenever he sees one of these new citizens, or hears fresh stories of their address and ability, Mr. Punch is proud and delighted. Perhaps in the past, even in the present, he may have been, or even still is, a little given to chaff Englishwomen for some of their foibles, and even their aspirations. But he never doubted how splendid they were at heart; he never for a moment supposed they would be anything but ready and keen when the hour of need struck.

July, 1916.

On the home front we have long been accustomed to the sound of guns, small and great, but it has come from training camps and inspires confidence rather than anxiety. We have been spared the horrors of invasion, occupation, wholesale devastation. In certain areas the noise of bombs and anti-aircraft guns has grown increasingly

Farmer (who has got a lady-help in the dairy): "'Ullo, Missy, what in the world be ye doin'?"
Lady: "Well, you told me to water the cows, and I'm doing it. They don't seem to like it much."

familiar, and on our south-east and east coasts war from the air, on the sea, and under the sea has become more and more audible as the months pass by. But July has brought us a new experience—the sound fifty or sixty miles inland in peaceful rural England, amid glorious midsummer weather, of the continual throbbing night and day of the great guns on the Somme, where our first great offensive opened on the 1st, and has continued with solid and substantial gains, some set-backs, heavy losses for the Allies, still heavier for the enemy. Names of villages and towns, which hitherto have been to most of us mere names on the map, have now become luminous through shining deeds of glory and sacrifice—Contalmaison and Mametz, Delville Wood, Thiepval and Beaumont-Hamel, Serre and Pozières.

The victory, for victory it is, has not been celebrated in the German way. England takes her triumphs as she takes defeats; without a sign of having turned a hair:

Yet we are proud because at last, at last
 We look upon the dawn of our desire;
Because the weary waiting-time is passed
 And we have tried our temper in the fire;
  And proving word by deed
Have kept the faith we pledged to France at need.

"Two heads with but a single thought"
First Head: "What prospects?"
Second Head: "Rotten."
First Head: "Same here."

But most because, from mine and desk and mart,
    Springing to face a task undreamed before,
Our men, inspired to play their prentice part
    Like soldiers lessoned in the school of war,
        True to their breed and name,
Went flawless through the fierce baptismal flame.

And he who brought these armies into life,
    And on them set the impress of his will—
Could he be moved by sound of mortal strife,
    There where he lies, their Captain, cold and still
        Under the shrouding tide,
How would his great heart stir and glow with pride!

The results of the battle of the Somme are shown in a variety of ways: by the reticence and admissions of the German Press, by its efforts to divert attention to the exploits of the commercial submarine cruiser *Deutschland*; above all, by the Kaiser's fresh explosions of piety. "The Devil was sick, the Devil a monk would be." There is no further sign of his fleet, which remains crippled by its "victory." Nor can he, still less his Ally, draw comfort from the situation on the Russian or Italian fronts.

Mr. Punch finds the usual difficulty in getting any details from his correspondents when they have been or are in the thick of the fighting. Practically all that they have to say is that there was a "damned noise," that breakfast was delayed by the "morning hate," or that an angry sub besought a weary O.C. "to ask our gunners not to serve faults into our front line wire." One of them, however, a very wise young man, ventures on the prediction that the War will last well into 1918. As the result of a brief leave he has learned an important truth. "In England they assume that you, having just arrived from France, *know*. When you return to France, it is assumed that you, having just arrived from England, *know*."

In Parliament Ireland is beginning to suffer from a rival in unenviable notoriety. Mesopotamia does not smell particularly sweet just now, but that may add to its usefulness as a red herring. Geographers are said to have some difficulty in defining its exact boundaries, but the Government are probably quite convinced that it is situate between the Devil and the Deep Sea. Two Special Commissions are to be set up to inquire into the Mesopotamian and Dardanelles Expeditions. Public opinion has been painfully stirred by the harrowing details which have come to light of the preventible sufferings endured by British troops. From their point of view the supply of their medical needs, now guaranteed, is worth a wilderness of Special Commissions. But Ireland still holds the floor, though Mr. Asquith is frugal of information as to the prospective Irish Bill and has deprecated discussion of the Hardinge Report, the most scarifying public document of our times. The Lords, unembarrassed by any

WELL DONE, THE NEW ARMY

embargo, have discussed the Report in a spirit which must make Mr. Birrell thank his stars that he got in his confession first. But why, he may ask, should he be judged by Lord Hardinge, himself a prospective defendant at the bar of public opinion?

Following the lead of a certain section of the Press, certain Members have begun to wax vocal on the subject of reprisals, uninterned Aliens, and the Hidden Hand. Their appeals to the Home Office to go on the spy-trail have not met with much

Conjurer (unconscious of the approach of hostile aircraft) "Now, Ladies and Gentlemen, I want you to watch me closely."

sympathy so far. An alleged Austrian taxi-driver has turned out to be a harmless Scotsman with an impediment in his speech. More interesting has been the sudden re-emergence of Mr. John Burns. He sank without a trace two years ago, but has now bobbed up to denounce the proposal to strengthen the Charing Cross railway-bridge. We could have wished that he had been ready to "keep the bridge" in another sense; but at least he has been a silent Pacificist. Mr. Winston Churchill, when his journalistic labours permit, has contributed to the debates, and Lord Haldane has again delivered his famous lecture on the defects of English education. But for Parliamentary sagacity *in excelsis* commend us to Mr. McCallum Scott. He is seriously perturbed about the shortage of sausage-skins and, in spite of the bland assurance of Mr. Harcourt that supplies are ample, is alleged to be planning a fresh campaign with the assistance of Mr. Hogge. Another shortage has given rise to no anxiety, but rather the reverse. In a police court it was recently stated that there are no longer any tramps in England. Evidently the appeal of that stirring old song, "Tramp! tramp! tramp! the boys are marching," has not been without its effect. Yet another endurable shortage is reported from the seaside, where an old sailor on the local sea front has been lamenting the spiritual starvation brought about by the war. "Why," he said, "for the first time for twenty years we ain't got no performing fleas down here." And performers, when they do come, are not always successful in riveting the attention of their audience.

August, 1916.

The third year of the War opens well for the Allies; so well that the Kaiser has again issued a statement denying that he is responsible for it. The Big Push on the Somme goes on steadily, thanks to fine leadership, the steadfast heroism of the New Armies; and the loyal co-operation of the munition-workers at home, who have deferred their holiday rather than hamper their brothers in the trenches by a lessened output.

Here one fact may suffice as a sample. The weekly consumption of high explosives by the Army is now between eleven and twelve thousand times as much as it was in September, 1914. Yet when a lieutenant is asked to state what it is really like being along with the B.E.F. when it is in its pushful mood, he sedulously eschews heroics, and will not commit himself to saying more than that it's all right—that he doesn't think there is any cause for anxiety. "We seem to have ceased to have sensations out here. It is a matter of business; the only question is how long is it going to take to complete." So, too, with the Tommies. "Wonderful," declares the man in the ranks to persistent seekers after thrilling descriptions of war. "You never see the like. Across in them trenches there was real soda-water in bottles." To return to our lieutenant, he "simply can't help being a little sorry for the Boche now that his wild oats are coming home to roost." Even his poetic friends, formerly soulful and precious, take this restrained view. The Attributes of the Enemy are thus summed up by one trench bard:

If Boches laughed and Huns were gents,
They'd own their share of continents;
There'd be no fuss, and, what is more,
There wouldn't even be a war.
Whereas the end of all this tosh
Can only be there'll be no Boche.

Another poet, an R.F.C. man, adopts the same vein, void alike of hate or exultation:

Returning from my morning fly
I met a Fokker in the sky,
And, judging from its swift descent,
It had a nasty accident.
On thinking further of the same
I rather fear I was to blame.

It is easy to understand why the enemy nations find England so disappointing and unsatisfying to be at war with.

The Big Push

Munition Worker: "Well, I'm not taking a holiday myself just yet, but I'm sending these kids of mine for a little trip on the Continent."

Italy, too, has had her Big Push on the Isonzo, capturing Monte Sabotino, which had defied her for fifteen months, and Gorizia—a triumph of scientific preparation and intrepid assault. The Austrian poison-gas attack on the Asiago plateau has been avenged, and the objectives of the long and ineffectual offensive of the previous winter carried with thousands of prisoners at a comparatively cheap price. To add to Austria's humiliation her armies on the Eastern Front have been placed under the Prussian Hindenburg. And Rumania has joined the Allies at the end of what has been a very bad month for the Central Empires. English newspapers have been excluded from Germany, and Berlin has added truthless to meatless days. But the Germans have long since found a substitute for veracity as well as for leather and butter and rubber and bread. They are said to have found a substitute for International Law, and it is an open secret that they are even now in search of a substitute for victory. We might even suggest a few more substitutes which have not yet been utilised. As, for example, a substitute for Verdun with the German flag flying over it; substitutes for several German Colonies; a substitute for Austria as an ally; and substitutes for Kultur and Organisation and Efficiency and World Power and the Mailed Fist and the Crown Prince and the Kaiser and the War and all the things that haven't come off.

Various momentous decisions have been arrived at in Parliament. The Cabinet are *not* to be cinematographed, and unnecessary taxi-whistling is to be suppressed, without any prejudice to the squealing of importunate chatterers below the gangway. Ireland has again dominated the Parliamentary scene; the Nationalists have resumed their freedom of action with attacks on Sir John Maxwell and martial law, and are displaying an embarrassing industry reminiscent of the 'Eighties. Mr. Ginnell has been removed by order of the Speaker; Mr. Duke has succeeded Mr. Birrell; and the discussion of three Irish Bills has bulked so large that one might almost forget we were at war. In such brief moments as could be spared from Irish affairs the Premier has proposed a fresh Vote of Credit for 450 millions, has introduced a Bill for extending the life of Parliament, and another establishing a new Register. The last has been unmercifully belaboured in debate, the Prime Minister himself describing it as "a halting, lopsided, temporary makeshift." The apparently insoluble problem is that of enabling soldiers in the trenches to exercise the franchise. Soldiers and sailors can very well wait for their votes, but not for their money, and the delays in providing pensions for discharged men have been condemned by members of all parties. So the War is not altogether forgotten by the House. Mr. Lloyd George, the new War Secretary, without wasting breath on the pessimistic comments of his colleague Mr. Churchill, has given an encouraging survey of the general situation. The cry has gone up that Mr. Hughes Must Come Back from Australia, and Mr. Swift MacNeill has been rewarded for his pertinacity by extracting a promise from Mr. Asquith that he will purge the Peerage of its enemy Dukes. Better still is the solemn assurance of the Premier that the Government are taking steps to discover the identity of all those who are in any way responsible for the judicial murder of Captain Fryatt—the worst instance of calculated atrocity against non-combatants since the murder of Nurse Cavell.

The education of our New Armies is full of strange and noble surprises. Now it is an ex-shop boy converted into an R.H.A. driver. Or again it is a Tommy learning to appreciate the heroism of a French peasant woman:

'Er bloke's out scrappin' with the rest,
    Pushin' a bay'net in Argonne;
She wears 'is photo on 'er breast,
    "Mon Jean," she sez—the French for John.

She 'ears the guns boom night an' day;
    She sees the shrapnel burstin' black;
The sweaty columns march away,
    The stretchers bringin' of 'em back.

She ain't got no war-leggin's on;
    'Er picture's never in the Press,
Out scoutin'. She finds breeks *"no bon,"*
    An' carries on in last year's dress.

At dawn she tows a spotty cow
    To graze upon the village green;
She plods for miles be'ind a plough,
    An' takes our washin' in between

She tills a patch o' spuds besides,
    An' burnt like copper in the sun,
She tosses 'ay all day, then rides
    The 'orse 'ome when the job is done.

The times is 'ard—I got me woes,
    With blistered feet an' this an' that,
An' she's got 'ers, the good Lord knows,
    Although he never chews the fat.

But when the Boche 'as gulped 'is pill,
    An' crawled 'ome to 'is bloomin' Spree,
We'll go upon the bust, we will,
    Madame an' Monsieur Jean an' me.

The Captain: "Your brother is doing splendidly in the Battalion. Before long he'll be our best man."
The Sister: "Oh, Reginald! Really, this is so very sudden."

Or once more it is the young officer shaving himself in a captured German dug-out before an old looking-glass looted from a *château* by a dead German, and apologising to its rightful owner:

> Madame, at the end of this long campaign,
> When France comes into her own again
> In the setting where only she can shine,
> As you in your mirror of rare design—
> > Forgive me, who dare
> > In a German lair
> To shave in your mirror at Pozières.

Then there are "lonely soldiers" in India, envious of their more fortunate comrades in Flanders, and soldiers quite the reverse of lonely during their well-earned leave.

Mistress (coming to maid's room as the Zeppelins approach): "Jane! Jane! Won't you come downstairs with the rest of us?"
Little Maid: "Oh, thank you, Mum, but I can see beautiful from here, Mum."

The education of those on the Home Front is also proceeding. There are some maids who announce the approach of Zeppelins as if they were ordinary visitors. There are others who politely decline to exchange a seat at an attic window for the security of the basement.

According to the German papers Prince Frederick Leopold of Prussia has been severely reprimanded by the Kaiser for permitting his wild swine to escape from their enclosure and damage neighbouring property. It would be interesting to know if Prince Leopold excused himself on the ground that he had merely followed the All Highest's distinguished example. When Princes are rebuked common editors cannot hope to escape censure. The editor of the *Vorwärts* has again been arrested, the reason given being that the newspaper does not truthfully represent Germany's position in the War. If the title of the organ is any indication of its contents the charge would appear to be more than justified.

September, 1916.

"Ian Hay" wrote a fine book on "The First Hundred Thousand"—the first batch of Kitchener's Army. Another book, equally glorious, remains to be written about another Hundred Thousand—the Sweepers of the Sea. And with them are to be reckoned the heroes of the little ships of whom we hear naught save the laconic record in a daily paper that "the small steamer —— struck a mine yesterday and sank," and that all the crew were lost:

> Who to the deep in ships go down,
>   Great marvels do behold,
> But comes the day when some must drown
>   In the grey sea and cold,
> For galleons lost great bells do toll,
>   But now we must implore
> God's ear for sunken Little Ships
>   Who are not heard of more.
>
> When ships of war put out to sea,
>   They go with guns and mail,
> That so the chance may equal be
>   Should foemen them assail;
> But Little Ships men's errands run,
>   And are not clad for strife;
> God's mercy, then, on Little Ships
>   Who cannot fight for life.
>
> To warm and cure, to clothe and feed,
>   They stoutly put to sea,
> And since that men of them had need
>   Made light of jeopardy;
> Each in her hour her fate did meet,
>   Nor flinched nor made outcry;
> God's love be with these Little Ships
>   Who could not choose but die.
>
> To friar and nun, and every one
>   Who lives to save and tend,
> Sisters were these whose work is done
>   And cometh thus to end;
> Full well they knew what risk they ran

But still were strong to give;
God's grace for nil the Little Ships
Who died that men might live.

September has brought us good tidings by land and air. Thiepval and Combles are ours, and the plague of the Zeppelins has been stayed. The downing of the Zepp at Cuffley by Lieutenant Robinson gave North London the most thrilling aerial spectacle ever witnessed. There has been much diversity of opinion as to the safest place to be in during a Zeppelin raid—under cover or in the open, on the top floor or in the basement; but recent experiences suggest that by far the most dangerous place on those occasions is in a Zeppelin. But perhaps the most momentous event of the month has been the coming of the Tanks, a most humorous and formidable addition to the fauna of the battlefield—half battleship, half caterpillar—which have given the Germans the surprise of their lives, a surprise all the more effective for being sudden and complete. The Germans, no doubt, have their surprise packets in store for us, but we can safely predict that they are not likely to be at once so comic and so efficient as these unlovely but painstaking monsters. As an officer at the front writes to a friend: "These animals look so dreadfully competent, I am quite sure they can swim. Thus, any day now, as you go to your business in the City, you may meet one of them trundling up Ludgate Hill, looking like nothing on earth and not behaving like a gentleman." As for the relations between the Allies in the field the same correspondent contributes some enlightening details. The French aren't English and the English aren't French, and difficulties are bound to arise. The course of true love never did run smooth. Here it started, as it generally does, with a rush; infatuation was succeeded by friction, and that in turn by the orthodox aftermath of reconciliation. "How do we stand now? We have settled down to one of those attachments which have such an eternity before them in the future that they permit of no gushing in the present." The War goes well on the Western Front, the worst news being the report that the Kaiser has undertaken to refrain in future from active participation in the conduct of military operations.

Peace reigns at Westminster, where legislators are agreeably conspicuous by their absence. But other agencies are active. According to an advertisement in the *Nation* the Fabian Research Department have issued two Reports, "together with a Project for a Supernatural Authority that will Prevent War." The egg, on the authority of the *Daily Mail*, is "disappearing from our breakfast table," but even the humblest of us can still enjoy our daily mare's nest. The effect of the Zeppelin on the young has already been shown; but even the elderly own its stimulating influence.

Above:

THE SWEEPERS OF THE SEA

Mr. Punch: "Risky work, isn't it?"

Trawler Skipper: "That why there's a hundred thousand of us doin' it."

Opposite:

THE REJUVENATING EFFECT OF ZEPPELINS

2 a.m. Crash!   Boom!   Bang!

Where is it?   I can't see it!   I must see it!

I will see it!   I shall see it!   Hooray!

October, 1916.

Mr. Punch's correspondents at the Front have an in corrigible habit of euphemism and levity. Even when things go well they are never betrayed into heroics, but adhere to the schoolboy formula of "not half bad," just as in the blackest hours they would not admit that things were more than "pretty beastly." Yet sometimes they deviate for a moment into really enlightening comment. No better summary of the situation as it stands in the third year of the War can be given than in the words of the faithful "Watch-dog," who has long been on duty in trench and dug-out and crater-hole:—

"This War has ceased to become an occupation befitting a gentleman—gentleman, that is, of the true Prussian breed. It was a happy and honourable task so long as it consisted of civilising the world at large with high explosive, poisonous gas and burning oil, and the world at large was not too ready to answer back. To persist in this stern business, in face of the foolish and ignoble obstinacy of the adversary, required great courage and strength of mind; but the Prussian is essentially courageous and strong. Things came to a pretty pass, however, when the wicked adversary made himself some guns and shells and took to being stern on his own. People who behave like that, especially after they have been conquered, are not to be mixed with—anything to keep aloof from such. One had to leave Combles, one had to leave Thiepval, one may even have to leave Bapaume to avoid the pest; these nasty French and English persons, with their disgusting tanks, intrude every where nowadays." The German engineer is being hoist with his own petard:

> Yet you may suck sweet solace from the thought
>> That not in vain the seed was sown,
> That half the recent havoc we have wrought
>> Was based on methods all your own;
> And smile to hear our heavy batteries
> Pound you with imitation's purest flatteries.

Yet, at best, this is sorry comfort for the Kaiser.

It is not a picnic for the men in our front line. Reports that the situation is "normal" or "quiet" or "uneventful" represent more or less correctly what is happening at G.H.Q., Divisional Headquarters, Brigade Headquarters, or even Battalion Headquarters. They represent understatement to the nth when applied to the front trenches. But listen again to the "Watch-dog." He admits that some of our diamonds are not smooth, but adds "for myself I welcome every touch of nature in these our warriors. It is good to be in the midst of them, for they thrive as never before, and their comforts are few enough these wet bloody days."

THE SUNLIGHT-LOSER

Kaiser (as his sainted Grandfather's clock strikes three): "The British are just putting their clocks back an hour. I wish I could put ours back about three years."

The Crown Prince, after seven months of ineffective carnage before Verdun, has been giving an interview to an American ex-clergyman, representing the Hearst anti-British newspapers, in which he appears in the light of a tender-hearted philanthropist, longing for peace, mercy, and the delights of home-life. Mr. Lloyd George, in an interview with an American journalist, has defined our policy as that of delivering a "knock out" to Prussian military despotism, a pugilistic metaphor which has wounded some of our Pacificists. Our Zeppelin bag is growing; Count Zeppelin has sworn to destroy London or die, but now that John Bull is getting his eye in, the oath savours of suicide.

The Allies have presented an ultimatum to Greece, but Mr. Asquith's appeal to the traditions of ancient Hellas is wasted on King Constantine, who, if he had lived in the days of Marathon and Salamis, would undoubtedly have been a pro-Persian. As for his future, Mr. Punch ventures on a prediction:

Tino, if some day Hellas should arise
    A phoenix soaring from her present cinders,
Think not to share her passage to the skies
    Or furnish purple copy for her Pindars;
You'll be in exile, if you don't take care,
Along with brother William, Lord knows where!

A couple of months ago, on the occasion of sharks appearing on the Atlantic coast of the U.S.A., it was freely intimated at the fashionable watering-places that there was such a thing as being too proud to bathe. Now a new and untimely irritant has turned up off the same shores in the shape of U-boats. Their advent is all the more inconsiderate in view of the impending Presidential Election, at which Mr. Wilson's claim is based on having kept America out of the War.

Members have returned to St. Stephen's refreshed by seven weeks' holiday, and the Nationalists have been recruiting their energies, but unfortunately nothing else, in Ireland. By way of signalising his restoration, after an apology, Mr. Ginnell handed in thirty-nine questions—the fruits of his enforced leisure. The woes of the interned Sinn Feiners who have been condemned to sleep in a disused distillery at Frongoch have been duly brought forward and the House invited to declare that "the system of government at present maintained in Ireland is inconsistent with the principles for which the Allies are fighting in Europe." The system of administration in Ireland is, and always has been, inconsistent with any settled principles whatsoever; but to propose such a motion now is equivalent to affirming that Ireland is being treated by Great Britain as Belgium and Poland and Serbia have been treated by Germany. Mr. Redmond made no attempt to prove this absurd thesis, but when he demanded that martial law should be withdrawn and the interned rebels let loose in a Home-ruled Ireland—while the embers of the rebellion were still dangerously smouldering—he asked too much even of that amicable and trustful beast, the British Lion. Mr. Duke

COMRADES IN VICTORY
Combles, September 26th
Poilu: "Bravo, mon vieux!"
Tommy: "Same to you, mate."

is not exactly a sparkling orator, but he said one thing which needed saying, namely, that Irishmen ought to work out a scheme of Home Rule for themselves, and lay it before Parliament, instead of expecting Englishmen to do their work for them and then complaining of the result. In the division-lobby the Nationalists received the assistance of some forty or fifty British Members, who supported the motion, Mr. Punch suspects, more out of hatred of the Coalition than of love for Ireland. But they were easily out-voted by British Home Rulers alone. The impression left by the debate was that the Nationalist Members had a great deal more sympathy with the Sinn Feiners than they had with the innocent victims of the rebellion.

The need of a War propaganda at home is illustrated by the answers to correspondents in the *Leeds Mercury*. "Reasonable questions" are invited, and here is one of the answers: "T.B.—No, it is not General Sir William Robertson, but the Rev. Sir William Robertson Nicoll who edits *The British Weekly*." But then, as another journal pathetically observes, "About nine-tenths of what we say is of no earthly importance to anybody." Further light is thrown on this confession by the claim of an Islington applicant for exemption: "Once I was a circus clown, but now I am on an evening newspaper."

We are grateful to Russia for her efforts, but, as our artist shows opposite, the plain person is apparently uncertain as to the quality of our Ally.

We are glad to learn that, on the suggestion of Mr. Asquith, the Lord Mayor's banquet will be "of a simple nature." Apropos of diet, an officer expecting leave writes "My London programme is fixed; first a Turkish bath, and then a nice fried sole." History repeats itself. A fried sole was the luxury which officers who served in the Boer War declared that they enjoyed most of all after their campaigning.

November, 1916.

Francis Joseph of Austria has died on the tottering throne which has been his for nearly seventy years. In early days he had been hated, but he had shown valour. Later on he had shown wisdom, and had been pitied for his misfortunes. It was a crowning irony of fate which condemned him in old age to become the dupe and tool of an Assassin. He should have died before the War—certainly before the tragedy of Sarajevo.

The British Push has extended to the Ancre, and the Crown Prince, reduced to the position of a pawn in Hindenburg's game, maintains a precarious hold on the remote suburbs of Verdun. Well may he be sick, after nine months of futile carnage, of a name which already ranks in renown with Thermopylæ.

As the credit of the Crown Prince wanes, so the cult of Hindenburg waxes.

Monastir has been recaptured by the Serbians and French; but Germany has had her victories too, and, continuing her warfare against the Red Cross, has sunk two hospital ships. Germany's U-boat policy is going to win her the War. At least so Marshal

Mother: "Come away, Jimmy! Maybe it ain't properly stuffed."

Hindenburg says, and the view is shared by that surprising person the neutral journalist. But in the mean time it subjects the affections of the neutral sailorman to a severe trial.

King Constantine, however, remains unshaken in his devotion to German interests. He has also shown marked originality by making up a Cabinet exclusively composed of University Professors. But some critics scent in his action a hint of compulsory Ministerial Service, and predict Labour troubles.

At home we have to note the steady set of the tide of public opinion in favour of Food Control. The name of the Dictator is not yet declared, but the announcement cannot be long postponed. Whoever he may be, he is not to be envied. We have also to note the steady growth on every side of Government bungalows—the haunts (if some critics are to be believed) of the Great Uncombed, even of the Hidden Hand. The men of forty-one were not wanted last March. Mr. Lloyd George tells us that they are wanted now, or it would mean the loss of two Army Corps. The Germans, by the way, appear to be arriving at a just conception of their relative value. Lord Newton has informed the Lords that the enemy is prepared to release 600 English civilian prisoners in return for some 4,000 to 7,000 Germans. Parliament has developed a new grievance: Ministers have confided to Pressmen information denied to M.P.s. And a cruel wrong has been done to Erin, according to Mr. Dillon, by the application of Greenwich time to Ireland, by which that country has been compelled to surrender its precious privilege of being twenty-

five minutes behind the times. The injustice is so bitter that it has reconciled Mr. Dillon and Mr. Healy.

The Premier has hinted that if the House insisted on having fuller information than it receives at present another Secret Session might be held. When one considers the vital problems on which Parliament now concentrates its energies—the supply of cocaine to dentists, the withholding of pictures of the Tanks, etc.—one feels that there should be a Secret Session at least once a week. Indeed, if the House were to sit permanently with closed doors, unobserved and unreported, the country might be all the better for it.

It is the fashion in some quarters to make out that fathers do not realise the sacrifice made by their sons, but complacently acquiesce in it while they sit comfortably at home over the fire. Mr. Punch has not met these fathers. The fathers—and still more the mothers—that he knows recognise only too well the unpayable nature of their debt.

> They held, against the storms of fate,
>   In war's tremendous game,
> A little land inviolate
>   Within a world of flame.
>
> They looked on scarred and ruined lands,
>   On shell-wrecked fields forlorn,
> And gave to us, with open hands,
>   Full fields of yellow corn;

Above:

A STRAIN ON THE AFFECTIONS

Norwegian (to Swede): "What—you here, too. I thought you were a friend of Germany?
Swede: "I was."

Opposite:

HINDENBURGITIS; OR, THE PRUSSIAN HOME MADE BEAUTIFUL

Pat (examining fare): "May the divil destroy the Germans!"
Sub: "Well, they don't do you much harm, anyway. You don't get near enough to 'em."
Pat: "Do they not, thin? Have they not kilt all the half-crown officers and left nothing but the shillin' ones?"

The silence wrought in wood and stone
    Whose aisles our fathers trod;
The pines that stand apart, alone,
    Like sentinels of God.

With generous hands they paid the price,
    Unconscious of the cost,
But we must gauge the sacrifice
    By all that they have lost.

The joy of young adventurous ways,
    Of keen and undimmed sight,
The eager tramp through sunny days,
    The dreamless sleep of night,

The happy hours that come and go,
    In youth's untiring quest,
They gave, because they willed it so,
    With some light-hearted jest.

No lavish love of future years,
    No passionate regret,
No gift of sacrifice or tears
    Can ever pay the debt.

Yet if ever you try to express this indebtedness to the wonderful young men who survive, they turn the whole thing into a jest and tell you, for example, that only two things really interest them, "Europe and their stomachs"—nothing in between matters.

Guy Fawkes Day has come and gone without fireworks, pursuant to the Defence of the Realm Act. Even Parliament omitted to sit. Apropos of Secret Sessions, Lord Northcliffe has been accused of having had one all to himself and some five hundred other gentlemen at a club luncheon. The *Daily Mail* describes the debate on the subject as a "gross waste of time," which seems to come perilously near *lèse-majesté!* But then, as a writer in the *Evening News*—another Northcliffe paper—safely observes, "It is the failing of many people to say what they think without thinking."

December, 1916.

Rumania has unhappily given Germany the chance of a cheap and spectacular triumph—of which, after being badly pounded on the Somme, she was sorely in need. Here was a comparatively small nation, whom the Germans could crush under their heel as they had crushed Belgium and Serbia. So in Rumania they concentrated all the men they could spare from other fronts and put them under their best generals. Their first plans were thwarted, but eventually the big guns had their way and Bukarest fell. Then, after the usual display of bunting and joy-bells in Berlin, was the moment to make a noble offer of peace. The German peace overtures remind one of Mr. Punch's correspondents of the American advertisement: "If John Robinson, with whose wife I eloped six months ago, will take her back, all will be forgiven."

The shadowy proposals of those who preach humanity while they practise unrestricted frightfulness have not deceived the Allies. They know, and have let the enemy know, that they must go on until they have made sure of an enduring peace by reducing the Central Empires to impotence for evil.

When Mr. Asquith announced in the House on December 4 the King's approval of Reconstruction, few Members guessed that in twenty-four hours he would have ceased to be Prime Minister and that Mr. Lloyd George would have begun Cabinet-making. There has been much talk of intrigue. But John Bull doesn't care who leads the country so long as he leads it to victory. And as for Certain People Somewhere in

THE RETURN OF THE MOCK TURTLE-DOVE

Kaiser
Bethmann-Hollweg } (breathlessly): "Well?"

The Bird: "Wouldn't even look at me!"

France, we shall probably not be far wrong in interpreting their view of the present change as follows:

Thank God, we keep no politicians here;
    Fighting's our game, not talking; all we ask
Is men and means to face the coming year
            And consummate our task.

Give us the strongest leaders you can find,
    Tory or Liberal, not a toss care we,
So they are swift to act and know their mind
            Too well to wait and see.

The ultimate verdict on Mr. Asquith's services to the State as Prime Minister for the first two and a half years of the War will not be founded on the Press Campaign which has helped to secure his downfall. But, as one of the most bitterly and unjustly assailed ex-Ministers has said, "personal reputations must wait till the end of the War." Meanwhile, we have a Premier who, whatever his faults, cannot be charged with supineness.

Mr. Bonar Law, the new Leader of the House, has made his first appearance as Chancellor of the Exchequer. Moving a further Vote of Credit for 400 millions, he disclosed the fact that the daily cost of the War was nearer six than five millions. In regard to the peace proposals he found himself unable to better the late Prime Minister's statement that the Allies would require "adequate reparation for the past and adequate security for the future." In lucidity and dignity of statement Mr. Asquith was certainly above criticism. Lord Devonport has been appointed Food Controller and warned us of rigours to come. The most thrilling speech heard at Westminster this month has been that of Major Willie Redmond, fresh from the invigorating atmosphere of the front. While some seventy odd Nationalist Members are mainly occupied in brooding over Ireland's woes, two are serving in the trenches—William Redmond and Stephen Gwynn, both of them middle-aged men. *O si sic omnes!*

Our wounded need all their patience to put up with the curiosity of non-combatants. A lady, after asking a Tommy on leave what the stripes on his arm were for, being told that they were one for each time he was wounded, is reported to have observed, "Dear me! How extraordinary that you should be wounded three times in the same place!" Even real affection is not always happily expressed.

The tenderness with which King Constantine is still treated, even after the riot in Athens in which our bluejackets have been badly mishandled, is taxing the patience of moderate men. Mr. Punch, for example, exasperated by the cumulative effect of Tino's misdeeds, has been goaded into making a formidable forecast of surrender or exit:

THE NEW CONDUCTOR
Opening of the 1917 Overture.

You say your single aim is just to use
 Your regal gifts for your beloved nation;
Why, then, I see the obvious line to choose,
 Meaning, of course, the path of abdication;
Make up your so-called mind—I frankly would—
To leave your country for your country's good.

"Have you brought me any souvenirs?"
"Only this little bullet that the doctor took out of my side."
"I wish it had been a German helmet."

The German Emperor was prevented from being present at the funeral of the late Emperor Francis Joseph by a chill. One is tempted to think that in a lucid interval of self-criticism William of Hohenzollern may have wished to spare his aged victim this crowning mockery.

Motto for Meatless Days: "The time is out of joint." This is a *raison de plus* for establishing an *Entente* in the kitchen and getting Marianne to show Britannia how to cook a cabbage.

January, 1917.

Though the chariots of War still drive heavily, 1917 finds the Allies in good heart—"war-weary but war-hardened." The long agony of Verdun has ended in triumph for the French, and Great Britain has answered the Peace Talk of Berlin by calling a War Conference of the Empire. The New Year has brought us a new Prime Minister, a new Cabinet, a new style of Minister. Captains of Commerce are diverted from their own business for the benefit of the country. In spite of all rumours to the contrary Lord Northcliffe remains outside the new Government, but his interest in it is, at present, friendly. It is very well understood, however, that everyone must behave. And in this context Mr. Punch feels that a tribute is due to the outgoing Premier. Always reserved and intent, he discouraged Press gossip to such a degree as actually to have turned the key on the Tenth Muse. Interviewers had no chance. He came into office, held it and left it without a single concession to Demos' love of personalia.

Germany has not yet changed her Chancellor, though he is being bitterly attacked for his "silly ideas of humanity"—and her rulers have certainly shown no change of heart. General von Bissing's retirement from Belgium is due to health, not repentance. The Kaiser still talks of his "conscience" and "courage" in freeing the world from the pressure which weighs upon all. He is still the same Kaiser and Constantine the same "Tino," who, as the *Berliner Tageblatt* bluntly remarks, "has as much right to be heard as a common criminal." Yet signs are not wanting of misgivings in the German people.

Mr. Wilson has launched a new phrase on the world—"Peace without Victory"; but War is not going to be ended by phrases, and the man who is doing more than any one else to end it—the British infantryman—has no use for them:

> The gunner rides on horseback, he lives in luxury,
> The sapper has his dug-out as cushy as can be,
> The flying man's a sportsman, but his home's a long way back,
> In painted tent or straw-spread barn or cosy little shack;
> Gunner and sapper and flying man (and each to his job say I)
> Have tickled the Hun with mine or gun or bombed him from on high,
> But the quiet work, and the dirty work, since ever the War began,
> Is the work that never shows at all, the work of the infantryman.
>
> The guns can pound the villages and smash the trenches in,
> And the Hun is fain for home again when the T.M.B.s begin,
> And the Vickers gun is a useful one to sweep a parapet,
> But the real work is the work that's done with bomb and bayonet.
> Load him down from heel to crown with tools and grub and kit,
> He's always there where the fighting is—he's there unless he's hit;
> Over the mud and the blasted earth he goes where the living can;
> He's in at the death while he yet has breath, the British infantry-man!
>
> Trudge and slip on the shell-hole's lip, and fail in the clinging mire—
> Steady in front, go steady! Close up there! Mind the wire!
> Double behind where the pathways wind! Jump clear of the ditch, jump clear!
> Lost touch at the back? Oh, halt in front! And duck when the shells come near!
> Carrying parties all night long, all day in a muddy trench,
> With your feet in the wet and your head in the rain and the sodden khaki's stench!
> Then over the top in the morning, and onward all you can—
> This is the work that wins the War, the work of the infantryman.

THE DAWN OF DOUBT
Gretchen: "I wonder if this gentleman really is my good angel after all!"

And if anyone should think that this means the permanent establishment of militarism in our midst let him be comforted by the saying of an old sergeant-major when asked to give a character of one of his men. "He's a good man in the trenches, and a good man in a scrap; but you'll never make a soldier of him." The new armies fight all

Cook (who, after interview with prospective mistress, is going to think it over):
"'Ullo! Prambilator! If you'd told me you 'ad children I needn't have troubled
meself to 'ave come."
The Prospective Mistress: "Oh! B-but if you think the place would otherwise suit you, I dare
say we could board the children out."

the harder because they want to make an end not of this war but of all wars. As for the
regulars, there is no need to enlarge on their valour. But it is pleasant to put on record
the description of an officer's servant which has reached Mr. Punch from France:
"Valet, cook, porter, boots, chamber-maid, ostler, carpenter, upholsterer, mechanic,
inventor, needlewoman, coalheaver, diplomat, barber, linguist (home-made), clerk,
universal provider, complete pantechnicon and infallible bodyguard, he is also a soldier, if a very old soldier, and a man of the most human kind."

Parliament is not sitting, but there is, unfortunately, no truth in the report that
in order to provide billets for 5,000 new typists and incidentally to win the War,
the Government has commandeered the Houses of Parliament. The *Times Literary
Supplement* received 335 books of original verse in 1916, and it is rumoured that Mr.
Edward Marsh may very shortly take up his duties as Minister of Poetry and the
Fine Arts. Mr. Marsh has not yet decided whether he will appoint Mr. Asquith or
Mr. Winston Churchill as his private secretary. Meanwhile, a full list of the private
secretaries of the new private secretaries of the members of the new Government
may at any moment be disclosed to a long suffering public.

THE RECRUIT WHO TOOK TO IT KINDLY

On the Home Front the situation shows that a famous literary critic was also a true prophet:

O Matthew Arnold! You were right:
We need more Sweetness and more Light;
For till we break the brutal foe,
Our sugar's short, our lights are low.

The domestic problem daily grows more acute. A maid, who asked for a rise in her wages to which her mistress demurred, explained that the gentleman she walked out with had just got a job in a munition factory and she would be obliged to dress up to him.

Maids are human, however, though their psychology is sometimes disconcerting. One who was told by her mistress not to worry because her young man had gone into the trenches responded cheerfully, "Oh, no, ma'am, I've left off worrying now. He can't walk out with anyone else while he's there."

February, 1917.

The rulers of Germany—the Kaiser and his War-lords—proclaimed themselves the enemies of the human race in the first weeks of the War. But it has taken two years and a half to break down the apparently inexhaustible patience of the greatest of the neutrals. A year and three-quarters has elapsed since the sinking of the *Lusitania*. The forbearance of President Wilson—in the face of accumulated insults, interference in the internal politics of the United States, the promotion of strikes and sabotage by the agents of Count Bernstorff—has exposed him to hard and even bitter criticism from his countrymen. Perhaps he over-estimated the strength of the German-American and Pacificist elements. But his difficulties are great, and his long suffering diplomacy has at least this merit, that if America enters the War it will be as a united people. Germany's decision to resort to unrestricted submarine warfare on February 1 is the last straw: now even Mr. Henry Ford has offered to place his works at the disposal of the American authorities.

Day by day we read long lists of merchant vessels sunk by U-boats, and while the Admiralty's reticence on the progress of the anti-submarine campaign is legitimate and necessary, the withholding of statistics of new construction does not make for optimism. Victory will be ours, but not without effort. The great crisis of the War is not passed. That has been the burden of all the speeches at the opening of Parliament from the King's downward.

Lord Curzon, who declared that we were now approaching "the supreme and terrible climax of the War," has spoken of the late Duke of Norfolk as a man "diffident about powers which were in excess of the ordinary." Is not that true of the British race as a whole? Only now, under the stress of a long-drawn-out conflict, is it discovering the variety and strength of its latent forces. The tide is turning rapidly in Mesopotamia. General Maude, who never failed to inspire the men under his command on the Western front with a fine offensive spirit, has already justified his appointment by capturing Kut, and starting on a great drive towards Baghdad.

On the Salonika front, to quote from one of Mr. Punch's ever-increasing staff of correspondents, "all our prospects are pleasing and only Bulgar vile." On the Western front the British have taken Grandcourt, and our "Mudlarks," encamped on an ocean of ooze, preserve a miraculous equanimity in spite of the attention of rats and cockroaches and the vagaries of the transport mule.

At home the commandeering of hotels to house the new Ministries proceeds apace, and a request from an inquiring peer for a comprehensive return of all the buildings requisitioned and the staffs employed has been declined on the ground that to provide it would put too great a strain on officials engaged on work essential to winning the War.

The criticisms on the late Cabinet for its bloated size have certainly not led to any improvement in this respect, and one of the late Ministers has complained that the Administration has been further magnified until, if all its members, including under-secretaries, were present, they would fill not one but three Treasury Benches. Already this is a much congested district at question-time and the daily scene of a great push. Up to the present there are, however, only thirty-three actual Ministers of the Crown, and their salaries only amount to the trifle of £133,000. The setting up of a War Cabinet, "a body utterly unknown to the law," has excited the resentment of Mr. Swift MacNeill, whose reverence for the Constitution (save in so far as it applies to Ireland) knows no bounds; and Mr. Lynch has expressed the view that it would be a good idea if Ireland were specially represented at the Peace Conference, in order that her delegates might assert her right to self-government.

England, in February, 1917, seems to deserve the title of "the great Loan Land." Amateurs of anagrams have found satisfaction in the identity of "Bonar Law" with "War Loan B." As a cynic has remarked, "in the midst of life we are in debt." But the champions of national economy are not happy. The staff of the new Pensions Minister, it is announced, will be over two thousand. It is still hoped, however, that there may be a small surplus which can be devoted to the needs of disabled soldiers. Our great warriors are in danger of being swamped by our small but innumerable officials.

The older Universities, given over for two years to wounded soldiers and a handful of physically unfit or coloured undergraduates, are regaining a semblance of life by the housing of cadet battalions in some colleges. The Rhodes scholars have all joined up, and normal academic life is still in abeyance:

Above:
THE LAST THROW

Opposite:
Head of Government Department (in his private room in recently commandeered hotel):
"Boy! Bring some more coal!"

In Tom his Quad the Bloods no longer flourish;
    Balliol is bare of all but mild Hindoos;
The stalwart oars that his used to nourish
    Are in the trenches giving Fritz the Blues,
        And many a stout D.D.
Is digging trenches with the V.T.C.

It is true that Mr. Bernard Shaw has visited the front. No reason is assigned for this rash act, and too little has been made of the fact that he wore khaki—just like an ordinary person. Amongst other signs of the times we note that women are to be licensed as taxi-drivers:

War has taught the truth that shines
Through the poet's noble lines:
"Common are to either sex
Artifex and *opifex*."

A new danger is involved in the spread of the Army Signalling Alphabet. The names of Societies are threatened. The dignity of Degrees is menaced by a code which converts B.A. into Beer Ack. Initials are no longer sacred, and the great T.P. will become Toc Pip O'Connor unless some Emma Pip introduces a Bill to prevent the sacrilege.

Above:

A PLAIN DUTY

"Well, good-bye, old chap, and good luck! I'm going in here to do my bit, the best way I can. The more everybody scrapes together for the War Loan, the sooner you'll be back from the trenches."

Opposite:

The Brothers Tingo, who are exempted from military service, do their bit by helping to train ladies who are going on the land.

March, 1917.

With the end of Tsardom in Russia, the fall of Baghdad, and the strategic retreat of
Hindenburg on the Western front, all crowded into one month, March fully maintains its reputation for making history at the expense of Cæsars and Kaisers. It seems
only the other day when the Tsar's assumption of the title of Generalissimo lent new
strength to the legend of the "Little Father." But the forces of "unholy Russia"—
Pro-German Ministers and the sinister figure of Rasputin—have combined to his
undoing, and now none is so poor to do him reverence. In the House of Commons
everybody seems pleased, including Mr. Devlin, who has been quite statesmanlike
in his appreciation, and the Prime Minister, in one of his angelic visits to the House,
evoked loud cheers by describing the Revolution as one of the landmarks in the
history of the world. But no one noticed that Sir Henry Campbell Bannerman's out-
burst in 1906, just after the dissolution of Russia's first elected Parliament: *"La Duma
est morte; vive La Duma!"* has now been justified by the event—at any rate for the
moment, for Revolutions are rich in surprises and reactions. The capture of Baghdad

ALSO RAN
Wilhelm: "Are you luring them on, like me?"
Mehmed: "I'm afraid I am!"

inspires no misgivings, except in the bosoms of Nationalist members, who detect in the manifesto issued by General Maude fresh evidences of British hypocrisy.

The fleet of Dutch merchantmen, which has been sunk by a waiting submarine, sailed under a German guarantee of "relative security." Germany is so often misunderstood. It should be obvious by this time that her attitude to International Law has always been one of approximate reverence. The shells with which she bombarded Rheims Cathedral were contingent shells, and the *Lusitania* was sunk by a relative torpedo. Neutrals all over the world, who are smarting just now under a fresh manifestation of Germany's respective goodwill, should try to realise before they take any action what is the precise situation of our chief enemy: He has (relatively) won the War; he has (virtually) broken the resistance of the Allies; he has (conditionally) ample supplies for his people; in particular he is (morally) rich in potatoes. His finances at first sight appear to be pretty heavily involved, but that soon will be adjusted by (hypothetical) indemnities; he has enormous (proportional) reserves of men; he has (theoretically) blockaded Great Britain, and his final victory is (controvertibly) at hand. But his most impressive argument, which cannot fail to come home to hesitating Neutrals, is to be found in his latest exhibition of offensive power, namely, in his (putative) advance—upon the Ancre.

A grave statement made by the Under-Secretary for War as to the recent losses of the Royal Flying Corps on the Western front and the increased activity of the German airmen has created some natural depression. The command of the air fluctuates, but the spirit of our airmen is a sure earnest that the balance will be redressed in our favour. Mr. Punch has already paid his tribute to the British infantryman. Let him now do his homage to the heroes whose end is so often disguised under the laconic announcement: "One of our machines did not return."

I like to think it did not fall to earth,
    A wounded bird that trails a broken wing,
But to the heavenly blue that gave it birth,
    Faded in silence, a mysterious thing,
Cleaving its radiant course where honour lies
Like a winged victory mounting to the skies.

The clouds received it, and the pathless night;
    Swift as a flame, its eager force unspent,
We saw no limit to its daring flight;
    Only its pilot knew the way it went,
And how it pierced the maze of flickering stars
Straight to its goal in the red planet Mars.

So to the entrance of that fiery gate,
    Borne by no current, driven by no breeze,
Knowing no guide but some compelling fate,
    Bold navigators of uncharted seas,
Courage and youth went proudly sweeping by,
To win the unchallenged freedom of the sky.

Parliament has been occupied with many matters, from the Report of the Dardanelles Commission to the grievances of Scots bee-keepers. The woes of Ireland have not been forgotten, and the Nationalists have been busily engaged in getting Home Rule out of cold storage. Hitherto every attempt of the British Sisyphus to roll the Stone of Destiny up the Hill of Tara has found a couple of Irishmen at the top ready to roll it down again. Let us hope that this time they will co-operate to install it there as the throne of a loyal and united Ireland. Believers in the "Hidden Hand" have been on the war-path, and as a result of prolonged discussion as to the responsibility for the failure of the effort to force the Dardanelles, the House is evidently of opinion that Lord Fisher might now be let alone by foes and friends. The idea of blaming *Queen Elizabeth* for the fiasco is so entirely satisfactory to all parties concerned that one wonders why the Commission couldn't have thought of that itself.

THE INFECTIOUS HORNPIPE

FOOD RESTRICTION
Scene: Hotel.
Little girl: "Oh. Mummy! They've given me a dirty plate."
Mother: "Hush, darling. That's the soup."

Mr. Bernard Shaw, returned from his "joy-ride" at the Front, has declared that "there is no monument more enduring than brass"; the general feeling, however, is that there is a kind of brass that is beyond enduring. Armageddon is justified since it has given him a perfectly glorious time. He is obliged, in honesty, to state that the style of some of the buildings wrecked by the Germans was quite second rate. He entered and emerged from the battle zone without any vulgar emotion; remaining immune from pity, sorrow, or tears. In short:

He went through the fiery furnace, but never a hair was missed
From the heels of our most colossal Arch-Super-Egotist.

According to the latest news from Sofia, 35,000 Bulgarian geese are to be allowed to go to Germany. As in the case of the Bulgarian Fox who went to Vienna, there appears to be little likelihood that they will ever return.

Apropos of food supplies, Lord Devonport has developed a sense of judicial humour, having approved a new dietary for prisoners, under which the bread ration will be cut down to 63 ounces per week, or just one ounce less than the allowance of the free and independent Englishman. The latest morning greeting is now: "*Comment vous Devonportez-vous?*"

April, 1917.

Once more the rulers of Germany have failed to read the soul of another nation. They thought there was no limit to America's forbearance, and they thought wrong. America is now "all in" on the side of the Allies. The Stars and Stripes and the Union Jack are flying side by side over the Houses of Parliament. On the motion introduced in both Houses to welcome our new Ally, Mr. Bonar Law, paraphrasing Canning, declared that the New World had stepped in to redress the balance of the old; Mr. Asquith, with a fellow-feeling, no doubt, lauded the patience which had enabled President Wilson to carry with him a united nation; and Lord Curzon quoted Bret Harte. The memory of some unfortunate phrases is obliterated by the President's historic message to Congress, and his stirring appeal to his countrymen to throw their entire weight into the Allied scale. The War, physically as well as morally, is now *Germania contra Mundum*. Yet, while we hail the advent of a powerful and determined Ally, there is no disposition to throw up our hats, The raw material of manpower in America is magnificent in numbers and quality, but it has to be equipped and trained and brought across the Atlantic. Many months, perhaps a whole year, must elapse before its weight can be felt on the battle front. The transport of a million men over submarine-infested seas is no easy task But while we must wait for the coming of the Americans on land, their help in patrolling the seas may be counted on speedily.

The British have entered Péronne; the Canadians have captured Vimy Ridge. But the full extent of German frightfulness has never been so clearly displayed as in their retreat. Here, for once, the German account of their own doings is true. "In the course of these last months great stretches of French territory have been turned by us into a dead country. It varies in width from 10 to 12 or 13 kilometres, and extends along the whole of our new positions. No village or farm was left standing, no road was left passable, no railway track or embankment was left in being. Where once were woods, there are gaunt rows of stumps; the wells have been blown up ... In front of our new positions runs, like a gigantic ribbon, our Empire of Death" (*Lokal Anzeiger*, March 18, 1917). The general opinion of the Boche among the British troops is that he is only good at one thing, and that is destroying other people's property. One of Mr. Punch's correspondents writes to say that while the flattened villages and severed fruit trees are a gruesome spectacle, for him "all else was forgotten in speechless admiration of the French people.

"Their self-restraint and adaptability are beyond words. These hundreds of honest people, just relieved from the domineering of the Master Swine, and restored to their own good France again, were neither hysterical nor exhausted." The names of the new German lines—Wotan and Siegfried and Hunding—are not without significance. We accept the omen: it will not be long before we hear of fresh German activities in the *Gotterdämmerung* line. Count Reventlow has informed the Kaiser that without victory a continuation of the Monarchy is improbable. The "repercussion" of Revolution is making itself felt. Even the Crown Prince is reported to have

The new-comer: "My village, I think?"
The one in possession: "Sorry, old thing; I took it half-an-hour ago."

felt misgivings as to the infection of anti-monarchial ideas, and Mr. Punch is moved to forecast possibilities of upheaval:

Not that the Teuton's stolid wits
    Are built to plan so rude a plot;
Somehow I cannot picture Fritz
    Careering as a *sans-culotte*;
Schooled to obedience, hand and heart,
    I can imagine nothing odder
Than such behaviour on the part
    Of inoffensive cannon-fodder.

And yet one never really knows.
    You cannot feed his massive trunk
On fairy tales of beaten foes,
    Or Hindenburg's "victorious" bunk;
And if his rations run too short
    Through this accursèd British blockade,
Even the worm may turn and sport
    A revolutionary cockade.

Above:
SWOOPING FROM THE WEST
(It is the intention of our new Ally to assist us in the patrolling of the Atlantic.)

Opposite:
DYNASTIC AMENITIES
Little Willie (of Prussia): "As one Crown Prince to another, isn't your Hindenburg line getting a bit shaky?"
Rupprecht (of Bavaria): "Well, as one Crown Prince to another, what about your Hohenzollern line?"

On the German Roll of Dishonour this month appears the name of one who has been *grande et conspicuum nostro quoque tempore monstrum.* Baron Moritz Ferdinand von Bissing, the German Military Governor-General of Belgium, who was largely responsible for the murder of Nurse Cavell and the chief instigator of the infamous Belgian deportations, after being granted a rest from his labours, is reported to have died "of overwork." Here for once we find ourselves in perfect agreement with the official German view. In a recent character sketch of the de ceased Baron, the *Cologne Gazette* observed, "He is a fine musician, and his execution was good." It would have been.

The proceedings in Parliament do not call for extended comment. Mr. Asquith has handsomely recanted his hostility to women's suffrage, admitting that by their splendid services in the war women have worked out their own electoral salvation.

Torpedoed mine-sweeper (to his pal): "As I was a-saying, Bob, when we was interrupted, it's my belief as 'ow the submarine blokes ain't on 'arf as risky a job as the boys in the airy-o-planes."

An old spelling-book used to tell us that "it is agreeable to watch the unparalleled embarrassment of a harassed pedlar when gauging the symmetry of a peeled pear." Lord Devonport, occupied in deciding on the exact architecture and decoration of the Bath bun (official sealed pattern), would make a companion picture. For the rest the House has been occupied with the mysteries of combing and re-combing. The best War saying of the month was that of Mr. Swift MacNeill, in reference to proposed peace overtures, that it would be time enough to talk about peace when the Germans ceased to blow up hospital ships.

Although the streets may have been sweetened by the absence of posters, days will come, it must be remembered, when we shall badly miss them. It goes painfully to one's heart to think that the embargo, if it is ever lifted, will not be lifted in time for most of the events which we all most desire—events that clamour to be recorded in the largest black type, such as "Strasbourg French Again," "Flight of the Crown Prince," "Revolution in Germany," "The Kaiser a Captive," and last and best of all, "Peace." But Mr. Punch, with many others, has no sympathy to spare for the sorrows of the head-line artist deprived for the time being of his chief opportunity of scaremongering.

In the competition; of heroism and self-sacrifice the prize must fall to the young— to the Tommy and the Second Lieutenant before all. Yet a very good mark is due to the retired Admirals who have accepted commissions in the R.N.R., and are mine-sweeping or submarine-hunting in command of trawlers. Yes, "Captain Dug-out, R.N.R.," is a fine disproof of *si vieillesse pouvait*.

According to the *Pall Mall Gazette*, Mr. Lloyd George's double was seen at Cardiff the other day. The suggestion that there are two Lloyd Georges has caused consternation among the German Headquarters Staff. But we are not exempt from troubles and anxieties in England. The bones of a woolly rhinoceros have been dug up twenty-three feet below the surface at High Wycombe, and very strong language has been used in the locality concerning this gross example of food-hoarding. The weather, too, has been behaving oddly. On one day of Eastertide there was an inch of snow in Liverpool, followed by hailstones, lightning, thunder, and a gale of wind. Summer has certainly arrived very early. But at least we are to be spared a General Election this year—for fear that it might clash with the other War.

May, 1917.

In England, once but no longer merry though not downhearted, in this once merry month of May, the question of Food and Food Production now dominates all others. It is the one subject that the House of Commons seems to care about. John Bull, who has invested a mint of money in other lands, realises that it is high time that he put something into his own—in the shape of Corn Bounties. Mr. Prothero, in moving the second reading of the Corn Production Bill, while admitting that he had originally been opposed to State interference with agriculture, showed all the zeal of the convert—to the dismay of the hard-shell Free Traders.

The Food Controller asks us to curtail our consumption of bread by one-fourth. Here, at least, non-combatants have an opportunity of showing themselves to be as good patriots as the Germans and of earning the epitaph: "Much as he loved the staff of life, he loved his country even more."

On the Western Front the German soldiers' opinion of "retirement according to plan" may be expressed as "each for himself and the Devil take the Hindenburg." One of them, recently taken prisoner, actually wrote, "When we go to the Front we become the worst criminals." This generous attempt to shield his superiors deserves to be appreciated, but it does not dispel the belief that the worst criminals are still a good way behind the German lines. The inspired German Press has now got to the point of asserting that "there is no Hindenburg line." Well, that implies prophetic sense:

And if a British prophet may
    Adopt their graphic present tense,
I would remark—and so forestall
    A truth they'll never dare to trench on—
There is no Hindenburg at all,
        Or none worth mention.

"No, dear, I'm afraid we shan't be at the dance to-night. Poor Herbert has got a touch of allotment feet."

According to our Watch Dog correspondent, recent movements show that the lawless German "has attained little by his destructiveness save the discomfort of H.Q. Otherwise the War progresses as merrily as ever; more merrily, perhaps, owing to the difficulties to be overcome. Soldiers love difficulties to overcome. That is their business in life." This is the way that young officers write "in the brief interludes snatched from hard fighting and hard fatigues." Their letters "never pretend to be more than the gay and cynical banter of those who bring to the perils of life at the Front an incurable habit of humour, and they are typical of that brave spirit, essentially English, that makes light of the worst that fate can send." That is how one brave officer wrote of the letters of a dead comrade to Punch only a few weeks before his own death.

A BAD DREAM

Spectre: "Well, if you don like the look of me, eat less bread."

HIS LATEST!
The Kaiser: "This is sorry work for a Hohenzollern; still, necessity knows no traditions."

The French have taken Craonne; saluting has been abolished in the Russian Army; and Germany has been giving practical proof of her friendliness to Spain by torpedoing her merchant ships. A new star has swum into the Revolutionary firmament, by name Lenin. According to the Swedish Press this interesting anarchist has been missing for two days, and it remains to be seen if he will yet make a hit. Meanwhile the Kaiser is doing his bit in the unfamiliar role of pro-Socialist.

Newmarket has become "a blasted heath," all horse-racing having been stopped, to the great dismay of the Irish members. What are the hundred thousand young men (or is it two ?), who refuse to fight for their country, to do? Mr. Lloyd George has produced and expounded his plan for an Irish Convention, at which Erin is to take a turn at her own harp, and the proposal has been favourably received, except by Mr. Ginnell, in whose ears the Convention "sounds the dirge of the Home Rule Act."

Mr. Bonar Law has brought in a Budget, moved a vote of credit for 500 millions, and apologised for estimating the war expenditure at 5½ millions a day when it turned out to be 7½. The trivial lapse has been handsomely condoned by his predecessor, Mr. McKenna. The Budget debate was held with open doors, but produced a number of speeches much more suitable for the Secret Session which followed, and at which it appears from the Speaker's Report that nothing sensational was revealed.

The House of Commons, unchanged externally, has deteriorated spiritually, to judge by the temper of most of those who have remained behind. It is otherwise with other Institutions, some of which have been ennobled by disfigurement.

A Place of Arms

I knew a garden green and fair.
   Flanking our London river's tide,
And you would think, to breathe its air
   And roam its virgin lawns beside,
All shimmering in their velvet fleece,
   "Nothing can hurt this haunt of Peace."

No trespass marred that close retreat;
   Privileged were the few that went
Pacing its walks with measured beat
   On legal contemplation bent;
And Inner Templars used to say:
"How well our garden looks to-day!"

But That which changes all has changed
   This guarded pleasaunce, green and fair,
And soldier-ranks therein have ranged
   And trod its beauties hard and bare,
Have tramped and tramped its fretted floor,
   Learning the discipline of War.

And many a moon of Peace shall climb
   Above that mimic field of Mars,
Before the healing touch of Time
   With springing green shall hide its scars;
But Inner Templars smile and say:
"Our barrack-square looks well to-day!"

Good was that garden in their eyes,
   Lovely its spell of long ago;
Now waste and mired its glory lies,
   And yet they hold it dearer so,
Who see beneath the wounds it bears
A grace no other garden wears.

For still the memory, never sere,
   But fresh as after fallen rain,
Of those who learned their lesson here
   And may not ever come again,
Gives to this garden, bruised and browned,
A greenness as of hallowed ground.

News comes from Athens that King Constantine is realising his position and contemplates abdication in favour of the Crown Prince George. It is not yet known in whose favour the Crown Prince George will abdicate. In this context the *Kölnische Zeitung* is worth quoting. "The German people," it says, "will not soon forget what they owe to their future Emperor." This spasm of candour is not confined to the Rhineland. The keenest minds in Germany, says a Berlin correspondent, are now seeking to discover the secret of the Fatherland's world-wide unpopularity. It is this absurd sensitiveness on the part of our cultured opponent that is causing some of her best friends in this country to lose hope.

Genius has been defined as an infinite capacity for taking pains; and if the definition is sound, genius cannot be denied to the painstaking officials who test the physical fitness of recruits—"as in the picture."

The month has witnessed the amendment of the President's much discussed phrase: "Too proud to fight" has now become "Proud to fight too." Another revised version is suggested by Margarine: *C'est magnifique, mais ce n'est as le beurre.* The German Food Controller laments the mysterious disappearance of five million four hundred thousand pigs this year. The idea of having the Crown Prince's baggage searched does not seem to have been found feasible.

OUR PERSEVERING OFFICIALS
Or, the Recruit that was passed at the thirteenth examination

June, 1917.

Within some eleven weeks of the Declaration of War by the U.S.A., the first American troops have been landed in France. Even the Kaiser has begun to abate his thrasonic tone, declaring that "it is not the Prussian way to praise oneself," and that "it is now a matter of holding out, however long it lasts."

But other events besides the arrival of the Americans have helped to bring about this altered tone. The capture of Messines Ridge, after the biggest bang in history, has given him something to think about. His brother-in-law, Constantine of Greece, has at last thrown up the sponge and abdicated. "Tino's" place of exile is not yet fixed. The odds seem to be on Switzerland, but Mr. Punch recommends Denmark. There is no place like home:

> Try some ancestral palace, well appointed;
>   For choice the one where Hamlet nursed his spite,
> Who found the times had grown a bit disjointed
>   And he was not the man to put 'em right;
> And there consult on that enchanted shore
>   The ghosts of Elsinore.

Brazil has also entered the War, and Germany is now able to shoot in almost any direction without any appreciable risk of hitting a friend.

Field-Marshal Sir Douglas Haig gave the nation a birthday present on his own birthday, in the shape of a dispatch which is as strong and straight as himself:

> Frugal in speech, yet more than once impelled
>   To utter words of confidence and cheer
> Whereat some dismal publicists rebelled
>   As premature, ill-founded, insincere—
> Words none the less triumphantly upheld
>   By Victory's verdict, resonantly clear,
> Words that inspired misgiving in the foe
>   Because you do not prophesy—you *know*.
>
> Steadfast and calm, unmoved by blame or praise,
>   By local checks or Fortune's strange caprices,
> You dedicate laborious nights and days
>   To shattering the Hun machine to pieces;
> And howsoe'er at times the battle sways
>   The Army's trust in your command increases;
> Patient in preparation, swift in deed,
> We find in you the leader that we need.

A new feature of the German armies are the special "storm-troops"; men picked for their youth, vigour, and daring, and fortified by a specially liberal diet for the carrying out of counter-attacks. Even our ordinary British soldiers, who are constantly compelled to take these brave fellows prisoners, bear witness to the ferocity of their appearance.

A WORD OF ILL OMEN

Crown Prince (to Kaiser, drafting his next speech): "For Gott's sake, father, be careful this time, and don't call the American Army 'contemptible.'"

On our Home Front the Germans have shown considerable activity of late. Daylight air-raids are no longer the monopoly of the South-east coast; they have extended to London. And a weekly paper, conspicuous for the insistence with which it proclaims its superiority to all others, has been asking: If 17 German aeroplanes can visit and bomb London in broad daylight, what is to prevent our enemy from sending 170 or even 1,700? Fortunately the average man and woman pays no heed to this scare-mongering, and goes about his or her business, if not rejoicing, at any rate in the conviction that the Gothas are not going to have it all their own way.

Considering that the "Fort of London" had been drenched with the "ghastly dew" of aerial navies barely three hours before Parliament met on June 13, Members showed themselves uncommon calm. They were at their best a few days earlier in paying homage to Major Willie Redmond. It had been his ambition to be Father of the House: he had been elected thirty-four years ago; but in reality he was the Eternal Boy from the far-off time when it was his nightly delight to "cheek" Mr. Speaker Brand with delightful exuberance until the moment of his glorious death in Flanders, whither he had gone at an age when most of his compeers were content to play the critic in a snug corner of the smoking-room. Personal affection combined with admiration for his gallantry to inspire the speeches in which Mr. Lloyd George, Mr. Asquith, and Sir Edward Carson enshrined the most remarkable tribute ever paid to a private Member.

Mr. Balfour has returned safe and sound from his Mission to the States, and received a warm welcome on all sides. Even the ranks of Tuscany, on the Irish benches, could not forbear to cheer their old opponent. Besides securing American gold for his country, he has transferred some American bronze to his complexion. If anything, he appears to have sharpened his natural faculty for skilful evasion and polite repartee by his encounter with Transatlantic journalists. In fact everybody is pleased to see him back except perhaps certain curious members, who find him even more chary of information than his deputy, Lord Robert Cecil. The mystery of Northcliffe's visit to the States has been cleared up. Certain journals, believed to enjoy his confidence, had described him as "Mr. Balfour's successor." Certain other journals, whose confidence he does not enjoy, had declined to believe this. The fact as stated, by Mr. Bonar Law is that "it is hoped that Lord Northcliffe will be able to carry on the work begun by Mr. Balfour as head of the British Mission in America. He is expected to co-ordinate and supervise the work of all the Departmental Missions." It has been interesting to learn that his lordship "will have the right of communicating direct with the Prime Minister"—a thing which, of course, he has never done before. Meanwhile, the fact remains that his departure has been hailed with many a dry eye, and that the public seem to be enduring their temporary bereavement with fortitude.

Far too much fuss has been made about trying to stop Messrs. Ramsay MacDonald and Jowett from leaving England. So far as we can gather they did not threaten to return to this country afterwards. There is no end to the woes of Pacificists, conscien-

Mrs. Green to Mrs. Jones (who is gazing at an aeroplane): "My word! I shouldn't care for one of *them* flying things to settle on me."

Stage manager: "The elephant's putting in a very spirited performance to-night."
Carpenter: "Yessir. You see, the new hind-legs is a discharged soldier, and the front legs is an out-and-out pacificist."

tious or otherwise. The Press campaign against young men of military age engaged in Government offices is causing some of them sleepless days. Even on the stage the "conchy" is not safe.

The King has done a popular act in abolishing the German titles held by members of his family, and Mr. Kennedy Jones has won widespread approval by declaring that beer is a food.

Lord Devonport's retirement from the post of Food Controller has been received with equanimity. There is a touch of imagination, almost of romance, in the appointment of his successor, the redoubtable Lord Rhondda, who as "D.A." was alternately the bogy and idol of the Welsh miners, and who, after being the head of the greatest profit-making enterprise in the Welsh coalfields, is now summoned to carry on war against the profiteers in the provision trade.

In Germany a number of lunatics have been called up for military service, and the annual report of one institution at Stettin states that "the asylums are proud that their inmates are allowed to serve their Fatherland." It appears, however, that the results are not always satisfactory, though no complaints have been heard on our side.

July, 1917.

The War, so Lord Northcliffe has informed the Washington Red Cross Committee, has only just begun. Whether this utterance be regarded as a statement of fact or an explosion of rhetoric, it has at least one merit. The United States cannot but regard it as a happy coincidence that their entry into the War synchronises with the initial operations. The dog-days are always busy times for the Dogs of War, and the last month of the third year opened with the new Russian Offensive under Brusiloff, and closed with the beginning of the Third Battle of Ypres. The War in the air and under the sea rages with unabated intensity, and in both Houses the policy of unmitigated reprisals on German cities has found strenuous advocates. But Lord Derby, our new Minister of War, will have none of it. British aeroplanes shall only be employed in bombing where some distinctly military object is to be achieved. But this decision does not involve any slackness in defensive measures. We have learned how to deal with the Zepp, and now we are going to attend to the Gotha. As for the U-boats, the Admiralty says little but does much. And we are adding to vigilance, valour, and the resources of applied science the further aid of agriculture.

In the old days the Kaiser was once described as "indefatigably changing Chancellors and uniforms." Dr. Bethmann-Hollweg has now gone the way of his greater predecessors—Bismarck and Caprivi, Prince Hohenlohe and Prince Büllow.

The Princes and the Peers depart, and the Doctors are following suit. Bethmann-Hollweg, immortalised by one fatal phrase, has been at last hunted from office by the extremists whom he sought to restrain, and Dr. Michaelis, a second-rate administrator, of negligible antecedents, succeeds to his uneasy chair, while the Kaiser maintains his pose as the friend of the people. He has congratulated his Bayreuth Dragoons on their prowess, which has given joy "to old Fritz up in Elysian fields":

> Perhaps; but what if he is down below?
> In any case, what we should like to know
> Is how his modern namesake, Private Fritz,
> Enjoys the fun of being blown to bits
> Because his Emperor has lost his wits.

Delirant reges: but there are bright exceptions. On July 17 our King in Council decreed that the Royal House should be known henceforth as the House of Windsor. Parliament has been flooded with the backwash of the Mesopotamia Commission, and at last on third thoughts the Government has decided not to set up a new tribunal to try the persons affected by the Report. Mr. Austen Chamberlain has resigned office amid general regret. The Government have refused, "on the representations of the Foreign Secretary," to accept the twice proffered resignation of Lord Hardinge. The plain person is driven to the conclusion that if there are no unsinkable ships there

Above:
THE TUBER'S REPARTEE
German Pirate: "Gott strafe England!"
British Potato: "Tuber über Alles!"

Opposite:
THE SCRAPPER SCRAPPED

are some unsinkable officials. For the rest the question mainly agitating Members has been "to warn or not to warn." The Lord Mayor has announced that he will not ring the great bell of St. Paul's; but the Home Secretary states that the public will be warned in future when an air raid is actually imminent.

During these visitations there is nothing handier than a comfortable and capacious Cave, but the Home Secretary has his limitations. When Mr. King asked him to be more careful about interning alien friends without trial, since he (Mr. King) had just heard of the great reception accorded in Petrograd to one Trotsky on his

SCRAPS OF PAPER AND OTHER RUBBISH MAY BE SHOT HERE BY ORDER BETHMANN-HOLLWEG

release from internment, Sir George Cave replied that he was sorry he had never heard of Trotsky.

Lord Rhondda reigns in Lord Devonport's place, and will doubtless profit by his predecessor's experience. It is a thankless job, but the great body of the nation is determined that he shall have fair play and will support him through thick and thin in any policy, however drastic, that he may recommend to their reason and their patriotism. This business of food-controlling is new to us as well as to him, but we are willing to be led, and we are even willing to be driven, and we are grateful to him

Busy city man to his partner (as one of the new air-raid warnings gets to work): "If you'll leave me in here for the warnings I'll carry on while you take shelter during the raids."

for having engaged his reputation and skill and firmness in the task of leading or driving us.

The War has its grandes heures, its colossal glories and disasters, but the tragedy of the "little things" affects the mind of the simple soldier with a peculiar force—the "little gardens rooted up, the same as might be ours"; "the little 'ouses all in 'eaps, the same as might be mine"; and worst of all, "the little kids, as might 'ave been our own." Apropos of resentment, England has lost first place in Germany, for America is said to be the most hated country now. The "morning hate" of the German family with ragtime obbligato must be a terrible thing! General von Blume, it is true, says that America's intervention is no more than "a straw." But which straw? The last?

It is reported that ex-King Constantine is to receive £20,000 a year unemployment benefit, and Mr. Punch, in prophetic vein, pictures him as offering advice to his illustrious brother-in-law:

Were it not wise, dear William, ere the day
   When Revolution goes for crowns and things,
To cut your loss betimes and come this way
   And start a coterie of exiled Kings?

In the words of a valued correspondent (a temporary captain suddenly summoned from the trenches to the Staff), "there is this to be said about being at war—you never know what is going to happen to you next."

Grandpapa (to small Teuton struggling with home-lessons): "Come, Fritz, is your task so difficult?"
Fritz: "It is indeed. I have to learn all the names of *all* the countries that misunderstand the All-Highest."

August, 1917.

With the opening of the fourth year of the War Freedom renews her vow, fortified by the aid of the "Gigantic Daughter of the West," and undaunted by the collapse of our Eastern Ally, brought about by anarchy, German gold and the fraternisation of Russian and German soldiers. The Kaiser, making the most of this timely boon, has once more been following in Bellona's train (her *train de luxe*) in search of cheap *réclame* on the Galician front, to witness the triumphs of his new Ally, Revolutionary Russia:

> But though she fail us in the final test,
>   Not there, not there, my child, the end shall be,
>   But where, without your option, France and we
> Have made our own arrangements in the West.

It is another story on the Western Front, where the British are closing in on the wrecked remains of Lens, and the Crown Prince's chance of breaking hearts along "The Ladies' Way" grows more and more remote.

Above:

RUSSIA'S DARK HOUR

Opposite:

THE OPTIMIST

"If this is the right village, then we're all right. The instructions is clear—Go past the post-office and sharp to the left afore you come to the church.'"

A recent resolution of the Reichstag has been welcomed by Mr. Ramsay MacDonald as the solemn pronouncement of a sovereign people, only requiring the endorsement of the British Government to produce an immediate and equitable peace. But not much was left of this pleasant theory after Mr. Asquith had dealt it a few sledge-hammer blows. "So far as we know," he said, "the influence of the Reichstag, not only upon the composition but upon the policy of the German Government, remains what it always has been—a practically negligible quantity."

The Reminiscences of Mr. Gerard, the late German Ambassador in Berlin, are causing much perturbation in German Court circles. In one of his conversations with Mr. Gerard, the Kaiser told him "there is no longer any International Law."

> Little scraps of paper,
>   Little drops of ink,
> Make the Kaiser caper
>   And the Nations think.

The real voice of Labour is not that of the delegates who want to go to the International Socialist Conference at Stockholm to talk to Fritz, but of the Tommy who, after a short "leaf," goes cheerfully back to France to fight him. And the fomenters of class hatred will not find much support from the "men in blue." Mr. Punch has had occasion to rebuke the levity of smart fashionables who visit the wounded and weary them by idiotic questions. He is glad to show the other side of the picture in the tribute paid to the V.A.D. of the proper sort:

There's an angel in our ward as keeps a-fiittin' to and fro,
With fifty eyes upon 'er wherever she may go;
She's as pretty as a picture, and as bright as mercury,
And she wears the cap and apron of a V.A.D.

The Matron she is gracious, and the Sister she is kind,
But they wasn't born just yesterday, and lets you know their mind;
The M.O. and the Padre is as thoughtful as can be,
But they ain't so good to look at as our V.A.D.

Not like them that wash a teacup in an orficer's canteen,
And then "Engaged in War Work" in the weekly Press is seen;
She's on the trot from morn to night and busy as a bee,
And there's 'eaps of wounded Tommies bless that V.A.D.

Our Grand Fleet keeps its strenuous, unceasing vigil in the North Sea. But we must not forget the merchant mariners now serving under the Windsor House Flag in the North Atlantic trade:

"We sweep a bit and we fight a bit—an' that's what we like the best—
But a towin' job or a salvage job, they all go in with the rest;
When we arn't too busy upsettin' old Fritz an' 'is frightfulness blockade
A bit all sorts don't come amiss in the North Atlantic trade."
"And who's your skipper, and what is he like?" "Oh, well, if you want to know,
I'm sailing under a hard-case mate as I sailed with years ago;
'E's big as a bucko an' full o' beans, the same as 'e used to be
When I knowed 'im last in the windbag days when first I followed the sea.
'E was worth two men at the lee fore brace, an' three at the bunt of a sail;
'E'd a voice you could 'ear to the royal yards in the teeth of a Cape 'Orn gale;
But now 'e's a full-blown lootenant, an' wears the twisted braid,
Commandin' one of 'is Majesty's ships in the North Atlantic trade."

"And what is the ship you're sailin' in?" "Oh, she's a bit of a terror.
She ain't no bloomin' levvyathan, an' that's no fatal error!

She scoops the seas like a gravy spoon when the gales are up an' blowin',
But Fritz 'e loves 'er above a bit when 'er fightin' fangs are showin'.
The liners go their stately way an' the cruisers take their ease,
But where would they be if it wasn't for us with the water up to our knees?
We're wadin' when theirsoles are wet, we're swimmin' when they wade,
For I tell you small craft gets it a treat in the North Atlantic trade!

Doctor: "Your throat is in a very bad state. Have you ever tried gargling with salt water?"
Skipper: "Yus, I've been torpedoed six times."

"An' what is the port you're plying to?" "When the last long trick is done
There'll some come back to the old 'ome port—'ere's 'opin' I'll be one;
But some 'ave made a new landfall, an' sighted another shore,
An' it ain't no use to watch for them, for they won't come 'ome no more.
There ain't no harbour dues to pay when once they're over the bar,
Moored bow and stern in a quiet berth where the lost three-deckers are.
An' there's Nelson 'oldin' 'is one 'and out an' welcomin' them that's made
The roads o' Glory an' the Port of Death in the North Atlantic trade."

Parliament has devoted many hours of talk to the discussion of Mr. Henderson's visit to Paris in company with Mr. Ramsay MacDonald to attend a Conference of French and Russian Socialists. As member of the War Cabinet and Secretary of the Labour Party he seems to have resembled one of those twin salad bottles from which oil and vinegar can be dispensed alternately but not together. The attempt to combine the two functions could only end as it began—in a double fiasco. Mr. Henderson has resigned, and Mr. Winston Churchill has been appointed Minister of Munitions. Many reasons have been assigned for his reinclusion in the Ministry. Some say that it was done to muzzle Mr. MacCallum Scott, hitherto one of the most pertinacious of questionists, who, as Mr. Churchill's private secretary, is now debarred by Parliamentary etiquette from the exercise of these inquisitorial functions. Others say it was done to muzzle Mr. Churchill. Contrary to expectation, Mr. Churchill has succeeded in piloting the Munitions of War Bill through its remaining stages in double quick time. Its progress was accelerated by his willingness to abolish the leaving certificate, which a workman hitherto had to procure before changing one job for another. Having had unequalled experience in this respect, he is convinced that the leaving certificate is a useless formality.

Food stocks going up, thanks to the energy of the farmers and the economy of consumers; German submarines going down, thanks to the Navy; Russia recovering herself; Britain and France advancing hand in hand on the Western Front, and our enemies fumbling for peace—that was the gist of the message with which the Prime Minister sped the parting Commons. "I have resigned," Mr. Kennedy Jones tells us, "because there is no further need for my services." Several politicians are of opinion that this was not a valid reason. A boy of eighteen recently told a Stratford magistrate that he had given up his job because he only got twenty-five shillings a week. The question of wages is becoming acute in Germany too, and it is announced that all salaries in the Diplomatic Service have been reduced. We always said that frightfulness didn't really pay.

September, 1917.

Thanks to the collapse of the Russian armies and "fraternisation," Germany has occupied Riga. But her chief exploits of late must be looked for outside the sphere of military operations. She has added a new phrase to the vocabulary of frightfulness—*spurlos versenkt*—in the instructions to her submarine commanders for dealing with neutral merchantmen. As for the position into which Sweden has been lured by allowing her diplomatic agents to assist Germany's secret service, Mr. Punch would hardly go the length of saying that it justifies the revision of the National Anthem so as to read. "Confound their Scandi-knavish tricks." But he finds it hard to accept Sweden's professions of official rectitude, and so does President Wilson.

PERFECT INNOCENCE

Constable Woodrow Wilson: "That's a very mischievous thing to do."

Sweden: "Please, sir, I didn't know it was loaded."

TRIALS OF A CAMOUFLAGE OFFICER

Sergeant-Major: "Beg pardon, sir, I was to ask if you'd step up to the battery, sir."

Camouflage Officer: "What's the matter?"

Sergeant-Major: "It's those painted grass screens, sir. The mules have eaten them."

The German Press accuses the United States of having stolen the cipher key of the Luxburg dispatches. It is this sort of thing that is gradually convincing Germany that it is beneath her dignity to fight with a nation like America. And the growing conviction in the United States that there can be no peace with the Hohenzollerns only tends to fortify this view in Court circles. The Kaiser's protestations of his love for his people become more strident every day.

In Russia the Provisional Government has been dissolved and a Republic proclaimed. If eloquence can save the situation, Mr. Kerensky is the man to do it; but so far the men of few words have gone farthest in the war. A "History of the Russian Revolution" has already been published. The pen may not be mightier than the sword to-day, but it manages to keep ahead of it.

With fresh enemy battalions, as well as batteries, constantly arriving from Russia, the Italians have been hard pressed, but their great assault on San Gabriele has saved the Bainsizza plateau. The Italian success has been remarkable, but the Russian collapse has prevented it from being pushed home. On the Western front no great events are recorded, but the mills of death grind on with ever-increasing assistance from the resources of applied science and the new art of *camouflage*. Yet the dominion of din and death and discomfort is still unable to impair our soldiers' capacity of extracting amusement from trivialities.

THE INSEPARABLE

The Kaiser (to his people): "Do not listen to those who would sow dissension between us. *I will never desert you.*"

The weather has been so persistently wet that it looks as if this year the Channel had decided to swim Great Britain. A correspondent, in a list of improbable events on an "extraordinary day" at the front, gives as the culminating entry, "It did not rain on the day of the offensive."

C.O. (to sentry): "Do you know the Defence Scheme for this sector of the line, my man?"
Tommy: "Yes, sir."
C.O.: "Well, what is it, then?"
Tommy: "To stay 'ere an' fight like 'ell."

When Parliament is not sitting and trying to make us "sit up," and when war news is scant, old people at home some times fall into a mood of wistful reverie, and contrast the Germany they once knew with the Germany of to-day.

A Lost Land

A childhood land of mountain ways,
Where earthy gnomes and forest fays,
Kind, foolish giants, gentle bears,
Sport with the peasant as he fares
Affrighted through the forest glades,
And lead sweet, wistful little maids
Lost in the woods, forlorn, alone,
To princely lovers and a throne.

Dear haunted land of gorge and glen,
Ah me! the dreams, the dreams of men!

A learned law of wise old books
And men with meditative looks,
Who move in quaint red-gabled towns,
And sit in gravely-folded gowns,
Divining in deep-laden speech
The world's supreme arcana—each
A homely god to listening youth,
Eager to tear the veil of Truth;

Mild votaries of book and pen—
Alas, the dreams, the dreams of men!

A music land whose life is wrought
In movements of melodious thought;
In symphony, great wave on wave—
Or fugue elusive, swift and grave;
A singing land, whose lyric rhymes
Float on the air like village chimes;
Music and verse—the deepest part
Of a whole nation's thinking heart!

Oh land of Now, oh land of Then!
Dear God! the dreams, the dreams of men!

Slave nation in a land of hate,
Where are the things that made you great?
Child-hearted once—oh, deep defiled,
Dare you look now upon a child?

Your lore—a hideous mask wherein
Self-worship hides its monstrous sin—
Music and verse, divinely wed—
How can these live where love is dead?

Oh depths beneath sweet human ken,
God help the dreams, the dreams of men!

The Norwegian explorer, Roald Amundsen, is preparing for a trip to the North Pole in 1918. Additional interest now attaches to this spot as being the only territory whose neutrality the Germans have omitted to violate. Apropos of neutrals, the crew of the U-boat interned at Cadiz has been allowed to land on giving their word of honour not to leave Spain during the continuance of the War. The mystery of how the word "honour" came into their possession is not explained. It is easier to explain that the Second Division, in which Mr. E. D. Morel is now serving, is not the one which fought at the battle of Mons.

October, 1917.

Another month of losses and gains. Against the break through at Caporetto on the Isonzo we have to set the steady advance of Allenby on the Palestine front, and the decision arrived at by an extraordinary meeting of German Reichstag members that the Germans cannot hope for victory in the field. We see nothing extraordinary in this. The Reichstag may not yet be able to influence policy, but it is not blind to facts—to the terribly heavy losses involved in our enemy's desperate efforts to prevent us from occupying the ridges above the Ypres-Menin road, and so forcing him to face the winter on the low ground. Then, too, there has been the ominous mutiny of the German sailors at Kiel. The ring leaders have been executed, but they may have preferred death to another speech from the Kaiser. Dr. Michaelis, that "transient embarrassed phantom," has joined the ranks of the dismissed. No sooner had the *Berliner Tageblatt* pointed out that "Dr. Michaelis was a good Chancellor as Chancellors go" than he went. Another of the German doctor politicians has been delivering his soul on the failure of Pro-German propaganda in memorable fashion. Dr. Dernburg, in *Deutsche Politik*, tells us that "steadfastness and righteousness are the qualities which the German people value in the highest degree, and which have brought it a good and honourable reputation in the whole world. When we make experiments in lies and deceptions, intrigue and low cunning, we suffer hopeless and brutal failure. Our lies are coarse and improbable, our ambiguity is pitiful simplicity. The history of the War proves this by a hundred examples. When our enemies poured all these things upon us like a hailstorm, and we convinced our selves of the effectiveness of such tactics, we tried to imitate them. But these tactics will not fit the German. We are rough but moral, we are credulous but honest." Before this touching picture of the German Innocents very much abroad, the Machiavellian Briton can only take refuge in silent amazement.

Parliament has reassembled, and Mr. Punch has been moved to ask Why? Various reasons would no doubt be returned by various members. The Chancellor of the Exchequer wants to obtain a further Vote of Credit. The new National Party wish to justify their existence; and those incarnate notes of interrogation—Messrs. King, Hogge and Pemberton Billing—would like Parliament to be in permanent session in order that the world might have the daily benefit of their searching investigations. There has been a certain liveliness on the Hibernian front, but we hope that Mr. Asquith was justified in assuming that the Sinn Fein excesses were only an expression of the "rhetorical and contingent belligerency" always present in Ireland, and that in spite of them the Convention would make all things right. Meanwhile, the Sinn Feiners have refused to take part in it. And not a single Nationalist member has denounced them for their dereliction; indeed, Mr. T. M. Healy has even given them his blessing, for what it is worth. Of more immediate importance has been Mr. Bonar Law's announcement of the Government's intention to set up a new Air Ministry, and "to employ our machines over German towns so far as military needs render us free to take such action."

In the earlier stages of the War we looked on the moon as our friend. Now that inconstant orb has become our enemy, and the only German opera that we look forward to seeing is *Die Gothadämmerung*. A circular has been issued by the Feline Defence League appealing to owners of cats to bring them inside the house during air-raids. When they are left on the roof it would seem that their agility causes them to be mistaken for aerial torpedoes. We note that the practice of giving air-raid warnings by notice published in the following morning s papers has been abandoned only after the most exhaustive tests. The advocates of "darkness and composure" have not been very happy in their arguments, but they are at least preferable to the members of Parliament deservedly trounced by Mr. Bonar Law, who declared that if their craven squeelings were typical he should despair of victory. Meanwhile, we have to congratulate our gallant French allies on their splendid bag of Zepps. But the space which our Press allots to air raids moves Mr. Punch to wonder and scorn. Our casualties from that source are never one-tenth so heavy as those in France on days when G.H.Q. reports "everything quiet on the Western front." Still worse is the temper of some of our society week lies, which have set their faces like flint against any serious

Above:
THE DANCE OF DEATH
The Kaiser: "Stop! I'm tired."
Death: "I started at your bidding; I stop when I choose."

Opposite:
A PLACE IN THE MOON
Hans: "How beautiful a moon, my love, for showing up England to our gallant airmen!"
Gretchen: "Yes, dearest, but may it not show up the Fatherland to the brutal enemy one of these nights?"

reference to the War, and go imperturbably along the old ante bellum lines, "snap-ping" smart people at the races or in the Row, or reproducing the devastating beauty of a revue chorus, and this at a time when every day brings the tidings of irreparable loss to hundreds of families.

Missing

"He was last seen going over the parapet into the German trenches."

What did you find after war's fierce alarms,
    When the kind earth gave you a resting-place,
And comforting night gathered you in her arms,
    With light dew falling on your upturned face?

Did your heart beat, remembering what had been?
    Did you still hear around you, as you lay,
The wings of airmen sweeping by unseen,
    The thunder of the guns at close of day?

All nature stoops to guard your lonely bed;
    Sunshine and rain fall with their calming breath;
You need no pall, so young and newly dead,
    Where the Lost Legion triumphs over death.

When with the morrow's dawn the bugle blew,
    For the first time it summoned you in vain,
The Last Post does not sound for such as you,
    But God's Reveille wakens you again.

The discomforts of railway travelling do not diminish. But impatient passengers may find comfort in a maxim of R. L. Stevenson: "To travel hopefully is a better thing than to arrive." And further solace is forthcoming in the fact that our enemies are even worse off than we are. Railway fares in Germany have been doubled; but it is doubtful if this transparent artifice will prevent the Kaiser from going about the place making speeches to his troops on all the fronts. Here all classes are united by the solidarity of inconvenience. And they all have different ways of meeting it. But we really think more care should be taken by the authorities to see that while waging war on the Continent they do not forget the defence of those at home. The fact that Mr. Winston Churchill and Mr. Horatio Bottomley were away in France at the same time looks like gross carelessness. In this context we may note the report that the Eskimos had not until quite recently heard of war, which seems to argue slackness on the part of the circulation manager of the *Daily Mail.*

Stout Lady (discussing the best thing to do in an air-raid): "Well. I always runs about meself. You see, as my 'usband sez, an' very reasonable too, a movin' targit is more difficult to 'it."

November, 1917.

The best and the worst news comes from the outlying fronts. Allenby's triumphant advance is unchecked in Palestine. Gaza has fallen. The British are in Jaffa. Jerusalem is threatened. The German-Austrian drive which began at Caporetto has been stemmed, and the Italians, stiffened by a British army under General Plumer, are standing firm on the Piave. In Mesopotamia we deplore the death of the gallant Maude, a great general and a great gentleman, beloved by all ranks, whose career is an abiding answer to those who maintain that no good can come out of our public schools or the Staff training of regular officers. In Russia the Bolshevist *coup d'état* has overthrown the Kerensky *régime* and installed as dictator Lenin, a *déclassé* aristocrat, always the most dangerous of revolutionaries. On the Western front the tide has flowed and ebbed. The Germans have yielded ground on the *Chemin des Dames*, the British have stormed Passchendaele Ridge, but at terrible cost, and General Byng's brilliant surprise attack and victory at Cambrai has been followed by the fierce reaction of ten days later. But perhaps the greatest sensation of the month has been Mr. Lloyd George's Paris speech, with its disquieting references to the situation on the Western front, and its announcement of the formation of the new Allied Council. The Premier's defence of, and, we may perhaps say, recomposition of his Paris oration before the House of Commons has appeased criticism without entirely convincing those who have been anxious to know how the Allied Council would work, and what would be the relations between the Council's military advisers and the existing General Staff of the countries concerned. But as Mr. Lloyd George confessed that he had deliberately made a "disagreeable speech" in Paris in order to get it talked about, the Press critics whom he rebuked will probably consider themselves absolved.

Parliament has for once repelled the gibe that it has ceased to represent the people in the tribute of praise paid by Lords and Commons to our sailors and soldiers and all the other gallant folk who are helping us to win the War. On the strength of this capacity for rising to the occasion one may pass over the many sittings at which a small minority of Pacificists and irrelevant inquisitors have dragged the House down to the depths of ineptitude or worse. In the debate on the Air Force in Committee, one member, if we count speeches and interruptions, addressed the House exactly one hundred times, and it is worthy of note that his last words were: "This is what you call muzzling the House of Commons." If we were to believe some critics, the British Navy is directed by a set of doddering old gentlemen who are afraid to let it go at the Germans, and cannot even safeguard it from attack. The truth, as expounded by the First Lord, Sir Eric Geddes, in his maiden speech, is quite different. Despite the Jeremiads of superannuated sailors and political longshoremen, the Admiralty is not going to Davy Jones's locker, but under its present chiefs, who have, with very few exceptions, seen service in this War, maintains and supplements its glorious record.

A GREAT INCENTIVE

Mehmed (reading dispatch from the All-Highest): "Defend Jerusalem at all costs for my sake. I was once there myself."

Save for an occasional game of "tip and run," as with the North Sea convoy, enemy vessels have disappeared on the surface of the ocean; and the long arm of the British Navy is now stretching down into the depths and up into the skies in successful pursuit of them. If the nation hardly realises what it owes to the men of the Fleet and their splendid comrades of the Auxiliary Services, it is because this work is done with such thoroughness and so little fuss, and, as Mr. Asquith put it, "in the twilight and not in the limelight."

One up!

Aunt Maria: "Do you know I once actually saw the Kaiser riding through the streets of London as bold as brass. If I'd known then what I know now I'd have told a policeman."

The general sense of the community is now practically agreed that compulsory rationing must come, and the sooner the better. Lord Rhondda is still hopeful that John Bull will tighten his own belt and save him the trouble. But if we fail, the machinery for compulsion is all ready.

Reuter reports that a British prisoner has been sentenced to a year's imprisonment for calling the Germans "Huns." On the Western front Tommy usually calls them "Allymans," "Jerry," or "Fritz." But even if this prisoner did use the word he cannot be blamed. The choice was the Kaiser's when, as Attila's understudy, "Go forth," he said, "my sons. Go and behave exactly as the Huns."

Apropos of the Kaiser, it appears that a certain Herr Stegerwald, addressing a Berlin meeting, said: "We went to war at the side of the Kaiser, and the All-Highest will return from war with us." If we may be permitted to say anything, we expect he will be leading by at least a couple of lengths.

The versatility and inventive genius of the Prime Minister provoke mingled comment. An old Parliamentarian, when asked to what party Mr. Lloyd George now belonged, recently answered: "He used to be a Radical; he will some day be a Conservative; and at present he is the leader of the Improvisatories."

December, 1917.

It seems useless to attempt to cope with the staggering multiplicity of events crowded into the last few weeks. Jerusalem captured in this last crusade, which realises the dream of Cœur de Lion; Russia "down and out" as a result of the armistice and the Brest-Litovsk Conference; Germany's last colony conquered in East Africa; Lord Lansdowne's letter; the retirement of Lord Jellicoe; while in one single week Cuba has declared war on Austria, the Kaiser has threatened to make a Christmas peace offer, and Mr. Bernard Shaw has described himself as "a mere individual." We have traversed the whole gamut of sensation from the sublime and tragic to the ridiculous; and Armageddon, vulgarised by the vulgar repetition of the journalist, has redeemed its significance in the dispatches from our Palestine front. The simplicity and dignity of General Allenby's entry into the Syrian town—

Where on His grave with shining eyes
The Syrian stars look down—

afford a happy contrast to the boastful pageantry of the Kaiser's visit in 1898. Meanwhile it has not yet been decided in Berlin what the Sultan of Turkey thinks of the capture of Jerusalem.

BETRAYED

The Pander: "Come on: come and be kissed by him."

Where Russia is concerned Mr. Balfour wisely declines to be included among the prophets; all he knows is that she has not yet evolved a Government with which we can negotiate.

There *is* a Government in Germany, but neither Government nor people afford excuse for the negotiations which Lord Lansdowne, in a fit of war-weariness, has advocated in his letter to the *Daily Telegraph*. His unfortunate intervention, playing into the hands of Pacificists and Pro-Boches, is all the more to be deplored in a public servant who has crowned a long, disinterested and distinguished career by an act of grievous disservice to his country. British grit will win, declares Sir William Robertson; but our elderly statesmen must refrain from dropping theirs into the machinery. Happily the Government are determined to give no more publicity to the letter than they can help. On the Vote of Credit for 550 millions the Chancellor of the Exchequer has been invited by Mr. Dillon to make a survey of the military situation, and has replied that all the relevant facts are known already. "The War is going on; the Government and the country intend it shall go on; and money is necessary to make it go on." That was a good answer to a member who has certainly done little to receive special consideration. Not only do we need money; we need men to supply the gaps caused by our withdrawal of troops to Italy and the constant wastage on all fronts.

Mr. Balfour, as we have seen, abstains from prophecy. Mr. Dillon, who, with other Nationalists, bitterly resents the decision of the Government to apply the rules of arithmetic to the redistribution of seats in their beloved country, has indulged in a terrifying forecast which ought to be placed on record. He has threatened the House with the possibility that at the next General Election he and his colleagues might be wiped out of existence.

Tommy is a very great man, but he is not a great linguist, though he always gets what he wants by the aid of signs or telepathy. Three years and some odd months have not changed his point of view, and now for Thomas to find himself in Italy is only to discover another lot of people who cannot understand or make themselves understood. "Alliances," as a correspondent from Italy puts it, "are things as wonderful to see as they are magnificent to read about. I do, however, regard with something approaching alarm the new language which will be evolved to put the lot of us on complete speaking terms."

Lord Rhondda, who listened from the Peers' gallery to the recent debate in the Commons on Food Control, has received a quantity of advice intended to help him in minding his p's and q's, particularly the latter. In China, we read in the *Daily Express*, a chicken can still be purchased for six-pence; intending purchasers should note, however, that at present the return fare to Shanghai brings the total cost to a figure a trifle in excess of the present London prices. More bread is being eaten than ever, according to the Food Controller; but it appears that the stuff is now eaten by itself instead of being spread thinly on butter, as in pre-war days. Bloaters have

THE NEED OF MEN

Mr. Punch (to the Comber-out): "More power to your elbow, sir. But when are you going to fill up that silly gap?"

Sir Auckland Geddes: "Hush! Hush! We're waiting for the Millennium."

reached the unprecedented price of sixpence each. This is no more, as we have seen, than a chicken fetches in China, but it is enough to dispel the hope that bloaters, at any rate over the Christmas season, would remain within the reach of the upper classes. At a Guildford charity fête the winner of a hurdle race has been awarded a new-laid egg. If he succeeds in winning it three years in succession it is to become his own property.

The new language
Tommy (to inquisitive French children) "Nah, then, alley toot sweet, an the tooter the sweeter!"

Christmas has come round again, and peace still seems a far-off thing. "What shall he have that killed the deer?" someone asks somebody else in *As You Like It*. But there is a better question than that, and it is this: "What shall they have that preserve the little dears?" And the answer is—honour and support. For there can be no doubt that in these critical times, when the life of the best and bravest and strongest is so cheap, no duty is more important than the cherishing of infancy, and the provision of seasonable joys to the youngest generation, gentle and simple. More than ever Mr. Punch welcomes the coming of Santa Klaus:

Thou who on earth was named Nicholas—
    There be dull clods who doubt thy magic power
    To tour the sleeping world in half-an-hour,
And pop down all, the chimneys as you pass,
    With woolly lambs and dolls of frabjous size
    For grubby hands and wonder-laden eyes.

Not so thy singer, who believes in thee
    Because he has a young and foolish spirit;
    Because the simple faith that bards inherit
Of happiness is still the master key,
    Opening life's treasure-house to whoso clings
    To the dim beauty of imagined things.

January, 1918.

While avoiding as a rule the fashionable *rôle* of prophet, Mr. Punch is occasionally tempted to indulge in prediction. The year 1918, in which France is greeting in increasing numbers the heirs of the Pilgrim Fathers, is going to be America's year. As for the Kaiser,

A Fatherland Poet was busy of late
In making the Kaiser a new Hymn of Hate;
Perhaps, ere its echoes have time to grow dim,
The Huns may be learning a new Hate of Him.

In this prophetic strain Mr. Punch has been musing on the fortunes of the Hohenzollerns under a German Republic. Will the ex-Kaiser be appointed to the post of official Gatherer of Scraps of Paper, or start in business as a second-hand wardrobe dealer with a large assortment of slightly soiled uniforms? Or will he be ordered to ring a joy-bell on the anniversary of the inauguration of the German Republic?

These are attractive speculations, but a trifle previous, while hospital ships are still being torpedoed, U-boats are busy at Funchal, and the bonds of German influence and penetration are being forged anew at Brest-Litovsk. The latest news from that quarter seems to indicate that the Kaiser desires peace—at any rate for the duration of the War. And already there is a talk of a German counter-offensive on a colossal scale on the Western front. So that Mr. Punch's message for the New Year is couched in no spirit of premature jubilation, but rather appeals for fortitude and endurance.

How needful such an appeal is may be gathered from the proceedings at Westminster, less fit for the Mother than the Mummy of Parliaments, where "doleful questionists" exhume imaginary grievances or display their "nerve" by claiming the increase in pay recently granted to fighting men for conscientious objectors in the Non-Combatant Corps. The interest taken by one of this group in Army Dentistry inspires the wish that "the treatment of jaw-cases," mentioned by the Under-Secretary for War could be applied on the Parliamentary front. Head-hunting is in full swing. This classical sport, as practised in Borneo, involved the discharge of poisoned darts through a blow-pipe, and the House of Commons has not materially altered the method. In the attack of January 23 it is supposed that the Head of the Government was aimed at; but most of the shots went wide and hit the Head of our Army in France. Ministers have not distinguished themselves except by their capacity for "butting-in" and eating their words. Public opinion has been inflamed rather than enlightened by the 'discussions on unity of command, and the newspaper campaign directed against our War chiefs. Meanwhile, the Suffragists have triumphantly surmounted their last obstacle in the House of Lords, and Votes for Women is now

The ex-Kaiser is appointed to the post of official gatherer of scraps of paper.

an accomplished fact. But the Irish Andromeda still awaits her Perseus, gazing wanly at her various champions in Convention. The Ulsterman's plea for conscription in Ireland has been rejected after Sir Auckland Geddes had declared that it would be of no use as a solution of the present difficulty. He did not give his reasons, but they are believed to be Conventional. Mr. Barnes has described the Government as "living on the top of a veritable volcano," but, in spite of the context, the phrase must not be taken to refer to the Minister of Munitions, who, as everybody knows, cannot be sat upon.

Military experts tell us that this is a "Q" war, meaning thereby that the Quartermaster-General's department is the one that matters. Naval experts sometimes drop hints attaching another significance to that twisty letter. Harassed house keepers are beginning to think that this is a "queue-war," and look to Lord Rhondda to end it. For the moment the elusive rabbit has scored a point against the Food Controller, but public confidence in his ability is not shaken. All classes are being drawn together by a communion of inconvenience. The sporting miner's wife can no longer afford dog biscuits: "Our dog's got to eat what we eats now." And the pathetic appeal of the smart fashionable for lump sugar, on the ground that her darling Fido cannot be expected to catch a spoonful of Demerara from the end of his nose, leaves the grocer cold. A dairyman charged with selling unsatisfactory milk has explained to the Bench that his cows were suffering from shell-shock. He himself is now suffering from shell-out-shock. At Ramsgate a shopkeeper h as exhibited a notice in his window announcing that "better days are in store." What most people want is butter days.

Above:
To all at home

Opposite:
Orderly Sergeant: "Lights out, there."
Voice from the hut: "It's the moon, Sergint."
Orderly Sergeant: "I don't give a d— what it is. Put it out!"

The disquieting activities of the "giddy Gotha" involve drastic enforcement of the lighting orders, and the moon is still an object of suspicion. Pessimists and those critics who are never content unless each day brings a spectacular success, seem to have taken for their motto: "It's not what I mean, but what I say, that matters." But the moods of the non-combatant are truly chameleonic. Civilians summoned to the War Office pass from confidence to abasement, and from abasement to megalomania in the space of half an hour.

Turkey, it appears, has sent an urgent appeal to Berlin for funds. The disaster to the *Goeben* can be endured, since the Sultan can now declare a foreshore claim, and do a little salvage profiteering; but Palestine is another matter. Since General Allenby's advance "running" expenses have swallowed up a formidable total. The War is teaching us many things, including geography. We are taking a lively interest in the Ukraine, and the newspapers daily add to our stock of interesting knowledge. Apropos of General Allenby's entry into Jerusalem, we learn that "the predominance of the tar brush in the streets added to the brightness of the scene," and in connection with his return to Cairo, that "the MacCabean Boy Scouts" took part in the reception—presumably the Cadet Corps of the Jordan Highlanders. But the most reassuring news comes from the enemy Press. "It is simply a miracle," says the *Cologne Gazette*, "that the Germans have so loyally stood by their leaders," and for once we are wholly in agreement with our German contemporary.

If Mr. Punch may exert his privilege of turning abruptly to grave from gay, the claim may be allowed on behalf of the youngest generation, already remembered in the chronicle of last month.

Children of Consolation

By the red road of storm and stress
   Their fathers' footsteps trod,
They come, a cloud of witnesses,
   The messengers of God.

Cradled upon some radiant gleam,
   Like living hopes they lie,
The rainbow beauty of a dream
   Against a stormy sky.

Before the tears of love were dried,
   Or anguish comfort knew,
The gates of home were opened wide
   To let the pilgrims through.

Pledges of faith, divinely fair,
   From peaceful worlds above
Against the onslaught of despair
   They hold the fort of love.

THE CIVILIAN AND THE WAR OFFICE

February, 1918.

"Watchman, what of the night?" The hours pass amid the clash of rumours and discordant voices—optimist, pessimist, pacificist. Only in the answer of the fighting man, who knows and says little, hut is ready for anything, do we find the best remedy for impatience and misgiving:

> "Soldier, what of the night?"
>> "Vainly ye question of me;
> I know not, I hear not nor see;
>> The voice of the prophet is dumb
> Here in the heart of the fight.
>> I count the hours on their way;
> I know not when morning shall come;
>> Enough that I work for the day."

The first Brest-Litovsk Treaty has been signed, followed in nine days by the German invasion of Russia, an apt comment on what an English paper, by a misprint which is really an inspiration, calls "the Brest Nogotiations."

The record of the Bolshevist régime is already deeply stained with the massacre of the innocents, but Lenin and Trotsky can plead an august example. More than fourteen thousand British non-combatants—men, women and children— have been murdered by the Kaiser's command. And the rigorous suppression of the strikes in Berlin furnishes a useful test of his recent avowals of sympathy with democratic ideals. By way of a set-off the German Press Bureau has circulated a legend of civil war in London, bristling with circumstantial inaccuracies. The enemy's successes in the field—the occupation of Reval and the recapture of Trebizond—are the direct outcome of the Russian *débâcle*. Our capture of Jericho marks a further stage in a sustained triumph of good generalship and hard fighting, which verifies an old prophecy current among the Arabs in Palestine and Syria, viz, that when the waters of the Nile flow into Palestine, a prophet from the West will drive the Turk out of the Arab countries. The first part of the prophecy was fulfilled by the pipe-line which has brought Nile water (taken from the fresh-water canal) for the use of the Egyptian Expeditionary Force across the Sinai desert to the neighbourhood of Gaza. The second part was fulfilled by the fact that General Allenby's name is rendered in Arabic by exactly the same letters which form the words "El Nebi," i.e. the Prophet.

At home we have seen the end of the seventh session of a Parliament which by its own rash Act should have committed suicide two years ago. Truly the Kaiser has a lot to answer for. On the last day but one of the session 184 questions were put, the information extracted from Ministers being, as usual, in inverse ratio to the curiosity

THE LIBERATORS

First Bolshevik: "Let me see; we've made an end of Law Credit, Treaties, the Army and the Navy. Is there anything else to abolish?"

Second Bolshevik: "What about War?"

First Bolshevik: "Good! And Peace too. Away with both of 'em!"

of the questioners. The opening of the eighth session showed no change in this respect. The debate on the Address degenerated into a series of personal attacks on the Premier by members who, not without high example, regard this as the easiest road to fame. The only persons who have a right to congratulate themselves on the discussion are the members of the German General Staff, who may not have learned anything that they did not know before, but have undoubtedly had certain shrewd suspicions confirmed. Mr. Bonar Law, in one of his engaging bursts of self-revelation, observed that he had no more interest in this Prime Minister than he had in the last; but the House generally seemed to agree with Mr. Adamson, the Labour leader, who, before changing horses again, wanted to be sure that he was going to get a better team. A week later, on the day on which the Prince of Wales took his seat in the Lords, Lord Derby endeavoured to explain why the Government had parted with Sir William Robertson, the Chief of the Imperial Staff, and replaced him by General Wilson. It is hard to say whether the Peers were convinced. Simultaneously in the House of Commons the Prime Minister was engaged in the same task, but with greater success. Mr. Lloyd George has no equal in the art of persuading an audience to share his faith in himself. How far our military chiefs approved the recent decision of the Versailles Conference is not known. But everyone applauds the patriotic self-effacement of Sir William Robertson in silently accepting the Eastern Command at home.

In Parliament the question of food has been discussed in both Houses with the greatest gusto. Throughout the country it is the chief topic of conversation. To the ordinary queues we now have to add processions of conscientious disgorgers patriotically evading prosecution. The problem "Is tea a food or is it not?" convulses our Courts, and the axioms of Euclid call for revision as follows:

"Parallel lines are those which in a queue, if only produced far enough, never mean meat."

"If there be two queues outside two different butchers' shops, and the length and the breadth of one queue be equal to the length and breadth of the other queue, each to each, but the supplies in one shop are greater than the supplies in the other shop, then the persons in the one queue will get more meat than those in the other queue, which is absurd, and Rhondda ought to see about it."

All the same, Lord Rhondda is a stout fellow who goes on his way with an imperviousness to criticism—criticism that is often selfish and contemptible—which augurs well for his ultimate success in the most thankless of all jobs.

Food at the front is another matter, and Mr. Punch is glad to print the tribute of one of his war-poets to the "Cookers":

The Company Cook is no great fighter,
    And there's never a medal for *him* to wear,
Though he camps in the shell-swept waste, poor blighter,
    And many a cook has "copped it" there;

Wife: "George, there are two strange men digging up the garden."
George: "It's all right, dear. A brainy idea of mine to get the garden dug up. I wrote an anonymous letter to the Food Controller and told him there was a large box of food buried there."
Wife: "Heavens! But there *is!*"

But the boys go over on beans and bacon,
    And Tommy is best when Tommy has dined,
So here's to the Cookers, the plucky old Cookers,
    And the sooty old Cooks that waddle behind.

"It is Germany," says a German paper, "who will speak the last word in this War." Yes, and the last word will be "Kamerad!" But that word will be spoken in spite of many pseudo-war-workers on the Home Front.

Among the many wonders of the War one of the most wonderful is the sailor-man, three times, four times, five times torpedoed, who yet wants to sail once more. But there is one thing that he never wants to do again—to "pal" with Fritz the square-head:

"When peace is signed and treaties made an' trade begins again,
There's some'll shake a German's 'and an' never see the stain;
"But *not me*," says Dan the sailor-man, "not me, as God's on high—
Lord knows it's bitter in an open boat to see your shipmates die."

Indignant war-worker: "And she actually asked me if I didn't think I might be doing something! Me? And I haven't missed a charity matinée for the last three months."

Among the ignoble curiosities of the time we note the following advertisements in a Manchester newspaper of "wants" in our "indispensable" industries: "Tennis ball inflators, cutters and makers" and "Caramel wrappers"; while a Brighton paper has "Wanted, two dozen living flies weekly during the remainder of winter for two Italian frogs."

The situation in Ireland remains unchanged, and suggests the following historical division of eras. (I) Pagan era; (2) Christian era; (3) De Valera.

March, 1918.

Once again the month of the War-God has been true to its name. March, opening in suspense, with the Kaiser and his Chancellor still talking of peace, has closed in a crisis of acute anxiety for the Allies. The expected has happened; the long-advertised German attack has been delivered in the West, and the war of movement has begun.

Breaking through the Fifth British Army, in five days the Germans have advanced twenty-five miles, to within artillery range of Amiens and the main lateral railway behind the British lines. Bapaume and Péronne have fallen. The Americans have entered the war in the firing line. It is the beginning of the end, the supreme test of the soul of the nation:

> The little things of which we lately chattered—
>   The dearth of taxis or the dawn of Spring;
> Themes we discussed as though they really mattered,
>   Like rationed meat or raiders on the wing;—
>
> How thin it seems to-day, this vacant prattle,
>   Drowned by the thunder rolling in the West,
> Voice of the great arbitrament of battle
>   That puts our temper to the final test.
>
> Thither our eyes are turned, our hearts are straining,
>   Where those we love, whose courage laughs at fear,
> Amid the storm of steel around them raining,
>   Go to their death for all we hold most dear.
>
> New-born of this supremest hour of trial,
>   In quiet confidence shall be our strength,
> Fixed on a faith that will not take denial
>   Nor doubt that we have found our soul at length.
>
> O England, staunch of nerve and strong of sinew,
>   Best when you face the odds and stand at bay;
> Now show a watching world what stuff is in you!
>   Now make your soldiers proud of you to-day!

Of our soldiers we at home cannot be too proud, from Field-Marshal to officer's servant. As one of Mr. Punch's correspondents at the front writes: "Dawn to me hereafter will not be personified as a rosy-fingered damsel or a lovely swift-footed

MADE IN GERMANY
Civilisation: "What's that supposed to represent?"
Imperial Artist: "Why, 'Peace,' of course,"
Civilisation: "Well, I don't recognise it—and I never shall."

deity, but as a sturdy little man in khaki, crimson-eared with cold, heralded and escorted by frozen wafts of outer air, bearing in one knobby fist a pair of boots, and in the other a tin mug of black and smoking tea." As for the charities and courtesies of war, as interpreted by our soldiers, Mr. Punch can wish for no better illustration than in these lines on "The German graves":

I wonder are there roses still
    In Ablain St. Nazaire,
And crosses girt with daffodil
    In that old garden there.
I wonder if the long grass waves
    With wild-flowers just the same,
Where Germans made their soldiers' graves
    Before the English came?

The English set those crosses straight
    And kept the legends clean;
The English made the wicket-gate
    And left the garden green;
And now who knows what regiments dwell
    In Ablain St. Nazaire?
But I would have them guard as well
    The graves we guarded there.

And when at last the Prussians pass
    Among those mounds and see
The reverent cornflowers crowd the grass
    Because of you and me,
They'll give, perhaps, one humble thought
    To all the "English fools"
Who fought as never men have fought
    But somehow kept the rules.

To turn from the crowning ordeal of our Armies to the activities of British politicians on the eve of the great German attack is not a soul-animating experience. Indeed, the efforts of Messrs. Snowden and Trevelyan, Pringle and King almost justify the assumption that Hindenburg would have launched his offensive earlier but for his desire not to interfere with the great offensive conducted by his friends on the Westminster front. Our anti-patriots, however, are placed in a dilemma. They were bound to side with Germany, because of their rooted belief that England always must be wrong. They were bound to hail the Bolshevik self-determinators because of

BY SPECIAL REQUEST
Customer: "Here, waiter, take a Coupon off this and ask the band to play five-penn'orth of
'The Roast Beef of Old England.'"

their entirely sound views on peace at any price. But now their two loves are fighting
like cats. Hence the problem: "Which am I (both can't well be right), Pro-German or
Pro-Trotskyite?" Discussions of pig shortage, commandeered premises, the relations
of the Government and Press, and the duties of the Directors of Propaganda leave us
cold or impatient. But members of all parties have been united in genuine grief over
the death of Mr. John Redmond, snatched away just when his distracted country
most needed his moderating influence. For in their anxiety not to interfere with the
deliberations of those patriotic Irishmen who are trying to settle how Ireland shall be
governed in the future, the Government are allowing it to become ungovernable by
anybody. A new and agreeable Parliamentary Innovation has been Introduced by Sir
Eric Geddes in the shape of an immense diagram showing the downward tendency
of the U-boat activities. Other orators might with advantage follow this method.
Indeed, there are some whose speeches would be more enjoyable if they were all dia-
grams. As for that pledge of the New Citizenship, the Education Bill, the debate on
the second reading has been such a long eulogy of its author that Mr. Fisher would
be well advised to offer a Propitiatory sacrifice to Nemesis.

Compulsory rationing is now an established fact, and the temporary disappearance of marmalade from the breakfast table has called forth many a *cri de cœur*. As
one lyrist puts it:

Let Beef and Butter, Rolls and Rabbits fade,
But give me back my love, my Marmalade.

And another has addressed this touching vow to margarine:

Whether the years prove fat or lean
    This vow I here rehearse:
I take you, dearest Margarine,
    For butter or for worse.

It is reported that the Government's standard suits for men's wear will soon be available. One is occasionally tempted to hope that women's costumes might be similarly standardised.

The German Press announces the death of the notorious "Captain of Koepenick," and the *Cologne Gazette* refers to him as "the only man who ever succeeded in making the German Army look ridiculous." This is the kind of subtle flattery that the Hohenzollerns really appreciate.

THE COAT THAT DIDN'T COME OFF

April, 1918

We have reached the darkest hours of the War and the clouds have not yet lifted, though the rate of the German advance has already begun to slow down. On the 11th the enemy broke through at Armentières and pushed their advantage till another wedge was driven into the British line. On the 12th Sir Douglas Haig issued his historic order: "With our backs to the wall, and believing in the justice of our cause, each one of us must fight to the end. The safety of our homes and the freedom of mankind depend alike upon the conduct of each one of us at the critical moment." The Amiens line being under fire, it was impossible to bring French reinforcements north in time to save Kemmel Hill and stave off the menace to the Channel ports. The tale of our losses is grievous, and for thousands and thousands of families nothing can ever be the same again. The ordeal of Paris has been renewed by shelling from the German long-distance gun, the last and most sensational of German surprise-packets. These are indeed dark days, yet already lit by hopeful omens—the closer union of the Allies, the appointment of the greatest French military genius, General Foch, as Generalissimo of the Allied Forces, and his calm assurance that we have as yet lost "nothing vital." America is pouring men into France and, without waiting to complete the independent organisation of her Army, has chivalrously sent her troops forward to be brigaded with French and British units. Even now there are optimists, who are not fools, who maintain that Germany has shot her last bolt and knows that she is losing. It is at least remarkable that German newspapers are daily excusing the failure of their offensive to secure all its objectives. There is clearly something wrong with the time-table and, in the race of Man Power, time is on the side of the Allies.

Truth, long gagged and disguised, is coming to light in Germany. This has been the month of the Lichnowsky disclosures—the Memoir of their Ambassador, vindicating British diplomacy and saddling Germany with the responsibility for the War. The time of publication is indeed unfortunate for the Kaiser, who has been telling us how bitterly he hates war.

> For now from German lips the world may know
>   Facts that should want some skill for their confounding—
> How Potsdam forced alike on friend and foe
>   A war of Potsdam's sole compounding.
>
> How you, who itched to see the bright sword lunged,
>   Still bleating peace like innocent lambs in clover,
> In all that bloody business you were plunged
>   Up to your neck and something over.

THE COMING ARMY
Father: "Here's to the fighter of lucky eighteen!"
Son: "And here's to the soldier of fifty!"

THE DEATH LORD
The Kaiser (on reading the appalling tale of German losses):
"What matter, so we Hohenzollerns survive?"

And, having fed on little else but lies,
   Your people, with the hollow place grown larger
Now that the truth has cut off these supplies,
   May want your head upon a charger.

And what has England's answer been, apart from the stubborn and heroic resistance of her men on the Western Front? The answer is to be found in the immediate resolve to raise the age limit for service to 50, still more in the glorious exploit of Zeebrugge and Ostend, in the incredible valour of the men who volunteered for and carried through what is perhaps the most astonishing and audacious enterprise in the annals of the Navy.

The pageantry of war has gone, but here at least is a magnificence of achievement and self-sacrifice on the epic scale which beggars description and transcends praise. The hornet's nest that has pestered us so long, if not rooted out, has been badly damaged; our sailors, dead and living, have once more proved themselves masters of the impossible.

At home Parliament, resuming business after the Easter recess, began by giving a second Reading to a Drainage Bill, and ended its first sitting in an Irish bog. Ireland throughout the month has dominated the proceedings, aloof and irreconcilable, brooding over past wrongs, blind to the issues of the War and turning her back on its realities. Mr. Lloyd George's plan of making Home Rule contingent on compulsory service has been described by Mr. O'Brien as a declaration of war on Ireland. Another Nationalist Member, who at Question time urged on the War Office the necessity of according to its Irish employees exactly the same privileges and pay as were given to their British confrères, protested loudly a little later on against a Bill which *inter alia* extends to Irishmen the privilege of joining in the fight for freedom. Mr. Asquith questioned the policy of embracing Ireland in the Bill unless you could get general consent. Mr. Bonar Law bluntly replied that if Ireland was not to be called upon to help in this time of stress there would be an end of Home Rule, and that if the House would not sanction Irish conscription it would have to get another Government. It remained for Lord Dunraven, before the passing of the Bill in the House of Lords, to produce as "a very ardent Home Ruler" the most ingenious excuse for his countrymen's unwillingness to fight that has yet been heard. Ireland, he tells us, has been contaminated by the British refugees who had fled to that country to escape military service.

The Prime Minister, in reviewing the military situation, has attributed the success of the Germans to their possessing the initiative and to the weather. Members have found it a little difficult to understand why, if even at the beginning of March the Allies were equal in numbers to the enemy on the West and if, thanks to the foresight of the Versailles Council, they knew in advance the strength and direction of the impending blow, they ever allowed the initiative to pass to the Germans. It is known that hundreds of thousands of men have been rushed out of England since the last week of March.

DRAKE'S WAY

Zeebrugge, St. George's Day, 1918

Admiral Drake (to Admiral Keyes): "Bravo, sir. Tradition holds. My men singed a King's beard, and yours have singed a Kaiser's moustache."

Why, if Sir Douglas Haig asked for reserves, were they not sent sooner? These mysteries will be resolved some day. Meanwhile General Trenchard, late chief of the Air Staff, and by general consent an exceptionally brilliant and energetic officer, has retired into the limbo that temporarily contains Lord Jellicoe and Sir William Robertson. But Lord Rothermere (Lord Northcliffe's brother), who still retains the confidence of Mr. Pemberton Billing, remains, and all is well. The enemy possibly thinks it even better. "At least we should keep our heads," declared Mr. Pringle during the debate on the Man-Power Bill. We are not sure about this. It depends upon the heads.

It is a pity that the "New Oxford Dictionary" should have so nearly reached completion before the War and the emergence of hundreds of new words, now inevitably left out. The Air service has a new language of its own, witness the conversation faithfully reported by an expert:

Scene: R.F.C. Club.

Time: Every Time.

First Pilot. Why, it's Brown-Jones!
Second Pilot. Hullo, old thing! What are you doing now?
First Pilot. Oh, I'm down at Puddlemarsh teaching huns—monoavros, pups and dolphins.
Second Pilot. I'm on the same game, down at Mudbank—sop two-seaters and camels. We've got an old tinside, too, for joy-riding.
First Pilot. You've given up the rumpety, then?
Second Pilot. Yes. I was getting ham-handed and mutton-fisted, flapping the old things every day; felt I wanted to stunt about a bit.
First Pilot. Have you ever butted up against Robinson-Smith at Mudbank? He was an ack-ee-o, but became a hun.
Second Pilot. Yes, he crashed a few days ago—on his first solo flip, taking off—tried to zoom, engine konked, bus stalled— sideslip—nose-dive. Not hurt, though. What's become of Smith Jones? Do you know?
First Pilot. Oh, yes. He's on quirks and ack-ws. He tried spads, but got wind up. Have you seen the new—?
Second Pilot. Yes, it's a dud bus—only does seventy-five on the ceiling. Too much stagger, and prop stops on a spin. Besides, I never did care for rotaries. Full of gadgets too.
First Pilot. Well, I must tootle off now. I'm flapping from Northbolt at dawn if my old airship's ready—came down there with a konking engine—plug trouble.
Second Pilot. Well, cheerio, old thing—weather looks dud—you're going to have it bumpy in the morning, if you're on a pup.
First Pilot. Bye-bye, you cheery old bean.
[*Exuent.*

THE POLITICIAN WHO ADDRESSED THE TROOPS

The Emperor Karl of Austria, by his recent indiscretions, is winning for himself the new title of "His Epistolic Majesty." His suggestion that France ought to have Alsace-Lorraine has grated on the susceptibilities of his brother Wilhelm. But a new fastidiousness is to be noted in the Teuton character. "Polygamy," says an article in a German review, "is essential to the future of the German race, but a decent form must be found for it."

May, 1918.

With the coming of May the Vision of Victory which had nerved Germany to her greatest effort seemed fading from her sight. With its last days we see them making a second desperate effort to secure the prize, capturing Soissons and the Chemin des Dames and pushing on to the Marne. This time the French have borne the burden of the onslaught, but Rheims is still held, the Americans are pouring in to France at the rate of 250,000 a month, and have proved their mettle at Cantigny, a small fight of great importance, as it "showed their fighting qualities under extreme battle conditions," in General Pershing's words, and earned the praise of General Debeney for the "offensive valour" of our Allies.

The British troops have met Sir Douglas Haig's appeal as we knew they would:

Their *will to win* let Boches bawl
    As loudly as they choose,
When once our back's against the wail
'Tis not our *wont to lose*.

Those who have gone back at the seventh wave are waiting for the tide to turn. To the fainthearted or shaken souls who contend that no victory is worth gaining at the cost of such carnage and suffering, these lines addressed "To Any Soldier" may serve as a solvent of their doubts and an explanation of the mystery of sacrifice:

If you have come through hell stricken or maimed,
    Vistas of pain confronting you on earth;
    If the long road of life holds naught of worth
And from your hands the last toil as been claimed;
If memories of horrors none has named
    Haunt with their shadows your courageous mirth
    And joys you hoped to harvest turn to dearth,
And the high goal is lost at which you aimed;

THE THREATENED PEACE OFFENSIVE
German Eagle (to British Lion): "I warn you—a little more of this obstinacy and you'll rouse
the dove in me!"

Think this—and may your heart's pain thus be healed—
    Because of me some flower to fruitage blew,
Some harvest ripened on a death-dewed field,
    And in a shattered village some child grew
To womanhood inviolate, safe and pure.
For these great things know your reward is sure.

The Germans have reached Sevastopol, but the Kaiser's Junior Partner in the South is
only progressing in the wrong direction. While Wilhelm is laboriously struggling to get
nearer the sea, Mehmed is getting farther and farther away from it. The attitude of Russia
remains obscure. Mr. Balfour tells us that it is not the intention of the Government
to appoint an Ambassador to Russia. But there is talk of sending out an exploration
party to find out just where Russia has got to. Russia, however, is not the only country
whose attitude is obscure. The Leader of the Irish Nationalist Party is reported to have
said to a New York interviewer: "We believe that the cause of the Allies is the cause of
Freedom throughout the world." At the same time, while repudiating the policy of the
Sinn Feiners, he admitted that he had co-operated with them in their resistance to the

demand that Ireland should defend the cause of Freedom. The creed of Sinn Fein—
"Ourselves Alone"—is at least more logical than that of these neutral Nationalists:

And is not ours a noble creed
    With Self uplifted on the throne?
Why should we bleed for others' need?
    Our motto is "Ourselves Alone."

Why prate of ruined lands out there,
    Of churches shattered stone by stone?
We need not care how others fare,
    We care but for "Ourselves Alone."

Though mothers weep with anguished eyes
    And tortured children make their moan,
Let others rise when Pity cries;
    We rise but for "Ourselves Alone."

Let Justice be suppressed by Might,
    And Mercy's seat be overthrown;
For Truth and Right the fools may fight,
    We fight but for "Ourselves Alone."

Meanwhile, the gentle Mr. Duke has retired from the Chief Secretaryship to the
Judicial Bench; Mr. Shortt, his successor, recently voted against conscription for
Ireland; Lord French, the new Viceroy, is believed to favour it. The appointments
seem to have been made on the cancelling-out principle, and are as hard to reconcile
as the ministerial utterances on the recent German push. Thus Mr. Macpherson
declared that the crisis came upon us like a thief in the night, while on the same day
Mr. Churchill observed that the German offensive had opened a month later than
we had calculated, and consequently our reserves in munitions were correspondingly
larger than they would have been. Anyhow, it is a good hearing that the lost guns,
tanks, and aeroplanes have all been more than replaced, arid the stores of ammunition completely replenished while at the same time munition workers have been
released for the Army at the rate of a thousand a day. These results have been largely
due to the wonderful work of the women, who turned out innumerable shells of
almost incredible quality—not like that depicted by our artist.

Mr. Bonar Law has brought in his Budget and asked for a trifle of 842 mil-
lions. We are to pay more for our letters, our cheques, and our tobacco. The Penny
Postage has gone, and the Penny Pickwick with it. For the rest we have had the
Maurice Affair, which looked like a means of resurrecting the Opposition but

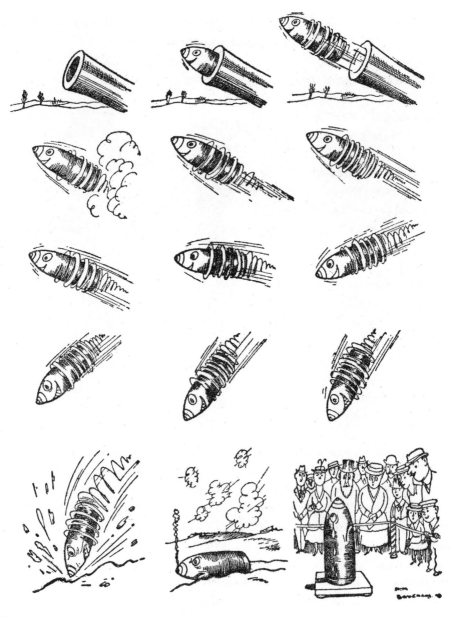

THE DUD

ended in giving the Government a new lease of life, and Sir Eric Geddes has given unexpected support to the allegations that the German pill-boxes were made of British cement. At least he admitted that the port of Zeebrugge was positively congested with shiploads of the stuff. Proportional Representation has been knocked out for the fifth time in this Parliament; and we have to thank Sir Mark Sykes for telling us that the Whip's definition of a crank is "a wealthy man

WOMAN POWER
Ceres: "Speed the plough!"
Ploughmen: "I don't know who you are, ma'am, but it's no good speeding the plough unless we can get the women to do the harvesting."
(Fifty thousand more women are wanted on the land to take the place of men called to the colours, if the harvest is to be got in.)

who does not want a Knighthood, or a nobleman who does not want to be an Under-Secretary."

War is a great leveller. The Carl Rosa Company are about to produce an opera by an English composer. And war is teaching us to revise our histories. For example, "'Nelson,' the greatest naval pageant film ever attempted, will," says the *Daily News*, "tell the love story of Nelson's life and the out standing incidents of his career, including the destruction of the Spanish Armada." No scandal about Queen Elizabeth, we trust. The *Daily News*, by the way, is much exercised by Mr. Punch's language towards the enemy, which it describes as being in the Billingsgate vein. In spite of which rebuke, and at the risk of offending the readers of that patriotic organ, Mr. Punch proposes to go on saying just what he thinks of the Kaiser and his friends.

The price of tobacco, as we have seen, is becoming a serious matter, but Ireland proposes to grapple with the problem in her own way. The Ballinasloe Asylum Committee, according to an announcement in the *Times* of May 14, have decided, with the sanction of the authorities, to grow tobacco leaf for the use of their inmates. "A doctor said that if the patients were debarred from an adequate supply of tobacco there would be no controlling them."

As a set-off to the anti-"Cuthbert" campaign in the Press the War Cabinet has in its Report declared that "the whole Empire owes the Civil Service a lasting debt of gratitude." It looks as if there was something in red tape after all. We must not, however, fail to recognise the growth of the new competitive spirit in the sphere of production, and Mr. Punch looks forward to the establishment of Cup Competitions for Clydesdale Riveters and London Allotment workers. Woman's work in munition factories has already been applauded; her services on the land are now more in need than ever.

June, 1918.

The danger is not past, but grounds for hope multiply. The new German assault between Montdidier and Noyon has brought little substantial gain at heavy cost. The attacks towards Paris have been held, and Paris, with admirable fortitude, makes little of the attentions of "Fat Bertha." "The struggle must be fought out," declared the Kaiser in the recent anniversary of his accession to the throne. In the meanwhile no opportunities of talking it out will be over looked by the enemy. He is once more playing the old game of striving to promote discord between the Allies. At the very moment when the official communiqués announced the capture of 45,000 prisoners, the Chancellor began a new peace offensive, aimed primarily at France, and supported by mendacious reports that the French Government were starting for Bordeaux, Clemenceau over thrown, and Foch disgraced. But the campaign of falsehood has proved powerless to shake France or impose on the German people. Commandeered enthusiasm is giving place to grave discontent. The awakening of Germany has begun, and the promise of a speedy peace falls on deaf ears. In the process of enlightenment the Americans have played a conspicuous part, in spite of the persistent belittlement of the military experts in the official German Press. The stars in their courses have some times seemed to fight for Germany, but they are withdrawing their aid.

THE CELESTIAL DUD

Kaiser: "Ha! A new and brilliant star added to my constellation of the Eagle!"

General Foch: "On the wane, I think."

(It in anticipated in astronomical circles that the new star, *Nova Aquilæ*, will shortly disappear.)

The long struggle between von Kühlmann and the generals has ended in the fall of the Minister; but not before he had indicated to the Reichstag the possibility of another Thirty Years' War, and asserted that no intelligent man ever entertained the wish that Germany should attain world-domination. There was a time when this frank reflection on the Hohenzollera intelligence would have constituted *lèse-majesté*. Coming from a Minister it amounts to a portent. Now he has gone, but the growing belief that military operations cannot end the war has not been scotched by his fall, and Herr Erzberger vigorously carries on the campaign against Chancellor Hertling and the generals. Austria has been at last goaded into resuming the offensive on the Italian Front and met with a resounding defeat. It remains to be seen how Turkey and Bulgaria will respond to the urgent appeals of their exacting master.

The ordeal of our men on the Western Front is terrible, but they have at least one grand and heartening stand-by in the knowledge that they have plenty of guns and no lack of shells behind them. This is the burden of the "Song of Plenty" from an old soldier to a young one:

The shelling's cruel bad, my son,
    But don't you look too black,
For every blessed German one
    He gets a dozen back—
But I remember the days
    When shells were terrible few
And never the guns could bark and blaze
    The same as they do for you.

But they sat in the swamp behind, my boy, and prayed for a tiny shell,
While Fritz, if he had the mind, my boy, could give us a first-class hell;
And I know that a 5.9 looks bad to a bit of a London kid,
But I tell you you were a lucky lad to come out when you did.

Up in the line again, my son,
    And dirty work, no doubt,
But when the dirty work is done
    They'll take the Regiment out—
But I remember a day
    When men were terrible few
And we hadn't reserves a mile away
    The same as there are for you,

But fourteen days at a stretch, my boy, and nothing about relief;
Fight and carry and fetch, my boy, with rests exceeding brief;

"COMPLETE ACCORD"; OR, ALL DONE BY KINDNESS
Imperial Trainer (to his dog Karl): "Now then, no nonsense: through you go!"

And rotten as all things sometimes are they're not as they used to be,
And you ought to thank your lucky star you didn't come out with me.

Our mercurial Premier lays himself open to a good deal of legitimate criticism, but for this immense relief, unstinted thanks are due to his energy and the devoted labours of the munition workers, women as well as men.

The Admiralty have decided not to publish the Zeebrugge dispatches for fear of giving information to the enemy. All he knows at present is that a score and more of his torpedo-boats, submarines, and other vessels have been securely locked up in the Bruges Canal by British Keyes. The Minister of Pensions has told the House the moving story of what has already been done to restore, so far as money and care can do it, the broken heroes of the War, and Lord Newton's alleged obstructiveness in regard to the treatment and exchange of prisoners has been discussed in the Lords. Mr. Punch's own impression is that Lord Newton owes his unmerited position as whipping boy to the fact that he does not suffer fools gladly, even if they come in the guise of newspaper reporters; and that, unlike his illustrious namesake, he has no use for the theory of gravity. Meanwhile the Kaiser, with a sublime disregard for sunk hospital-ships and bombed hospitals, continues to exhibit his bleeding heart to an astonished world.

Now that the Food Controller has got into his stride, the nation has begun to realise the huge debt it owes to his firmness and organising ability, and is proportionately concerned to hear of his breakdown from overwork. The queues have disappeared, supplies are adequate, and there are no complaints of class-favouritism.

It is remarkable how the British soldier will pick up languages, or at least learn to interpret them. Only last week an American corporal stopped a British Sergeant and said: "Say, Steve, can you put me wise where I can barge into a boiled-shirt biscuit-juggler who would get me some eats?" And the Sergeant at once directed him to a café. The training of the new armies, to judge by the example depicted by our artist, affords fresh proof of the saying that love is a *liberal* education.

The situation on the Parliamentary Front has been fairly quiet. The popular pastime of asking when the promised Home Rule Bill is to be introduced is no longer met by suitably, varied but invariably evasive replies. The Government has now frankly admitted that the policy of running Home Rule and Conscription in double harness has been abandoned, and expects better things from the new pair: Firm Government and Voluntary Recruiting. But sceptics are unconvinced that the Government will abandon the leniency prompted by "the insane view of creating an atmosphere in which something incomprehensible is to occur."

The lavish and, in many cases, inexplicable distribution of the Order of the British Empire bids fair to add a peculiar lustre to the undecorated. The War has produced no stranger paradox than the case of the gentleman who within the space of seven days was sentenced to six months' imprisonment for a breach of the Defence of the Realm regulations and recommended for the O.B.E. on account

A Pitiful Pose

Teuton crocodile: "I do so feel for the poor British wounded, I only wish we could do more for them."

("We Germans will preserve our conception of Christian duty towards the sick and wounded"
—*From recent remarks of the Kaiser reported by a German correspondent.*)

Bobby (at the conclusion of dinner): "Mother, I don't know how it is, but I never seem to get that—that——nice sick feeling nowadays."

Mistress (as the new troops go by): "Which of them is your cousin?"
Nursemaid (unguardedly): "I don't know yet, ma'am."

of good services to the country. The fact that the recommendation was withdrawn hardly justified the assumption of a Pacificist Member that a sentence under the Defence of the Realm Act was regarded as the higher honour of the two.

There is one thing, however, that war at its worst cannot do. It cannot make an Englishman forgo that peculiar and blessed birthright which enables him to over-throw the Giant Despair with the weapon of whimsical humour—in other words, to write, as a young officer has written for Mr. Punch, such a Let of verses as the following in June, 1918:

The Best Smell of All

When noses first were carved for men
    Of varied width and height,
Strange smells and sweet were fashioned then
    That all might know delight—
Smells for the hooked, the snub, the fine,
    The pug, the gross, the small,
A smell for each, and one divine
    Last smell to soothe them all.

The baccy smell, the smell of peat,
    The rough gruff smell of tweed,
The rain smell on a dusty street
    Are all good smells indeed;
The sea smell smelt through resinous trees,
    The smell of burning wood,
The saintly smell of dairies—these
    Are all rich smells and good.

And good the smell the nose receives
    From new-baked loaves, from hops,
From churches, from decaying leaves,
    From pinks, from grocers' shops;
And smells of rare and fine bouquet
    Proceed, the world allows,
From petrol, roses, cellars, hay,
    Scrubbed planks, hot gin and cows.

But there's a smell that doth excel
    All other smells by far,
Even the tawny stable smell

Or the boisterous smell of tar;
A smell stupendous, past compare,
    The king of smells, the prize,
That smell which floods the startled air
    When home-cured bacon fries!

All other smells, w'hate'er their worth,
    Though dear and richly prized,
Are earthy smells and of the earth,
    Are smells disparadised;
But when that smell of smells awakes
    From ham of perfect cure,
It lifts the heart to heaven and makes
    The doom of Satan sure.

How good to sit at twilight's close
    In a warm inn and feel
That marvellous smell caress the nose
    With promise of a meal!
How good when bell for breakfast rings
    To pause, while tripping down,
And snuff and snuff till Fancy brings
    All Arcady to Town!

But best, when day's first glimmerings break
    Through curtains half withdrawn,
To lie and smell it, scarce awake,
    In some great farm at dawn;
Cocks crow, the milkmaid clanks the pails,
    The housemaid bangs the stairs;
And BACON suddenly assails
    The nostrils unawares.

Noses of varied width and height
    Doth kindly Heaven bestow,
And choice of smells for our delight,
    That all some joy may know;
Noses and smells for all the race
    That on this earth do dwell,
And for a final act of grace
    The astounding bacon smell.

But the War has its drawbacks, and owing to its unexpected prolongation there is a rumour that Mr. H. G. Wells will readjust his ideas on the subject quarterly instead of twice a week as before.

July, 1918.

"France's Day" was held on July 14 under the auspices of the British Red Cross Committee. But this has been France's month, the month in which the miracle of the first battle of the Marne has been equalled by the second and the Germans have been hurled back across the fatal river by the tremendous counterstroke of General Foch.

On the 15th the Germans launched their great offensive. On the 20th they recrossed the Marne, and are now entitled to complain that General Foch not only took over the French and British armies, but has recently started taking over a good part of the German army. The neighbourhood has never been a healthy one for the Huns since the days of Attila.

Fritz has crossed the Marne and recrossed it—according to plan—and is already on the way to the Aisne. The battle of the rivers has begun again, but on new lines. Yet this amazing turn of the tide has been taken very quietly in France and England. The Allies have rung no joy-bells; they are content with doing their best to give Germany no occasion for further indulgence in that form of jubilation. And Germany is meeting them more than half way, their authorities having ordered a supplementary requisition of those church-bells which were exempted when the first confiscation was made. "At this heavy hour," said von Kühlmann to the Reichstag, "none of us fully realise what we owe to the German Emperor." That was a month ago; the realisation of their indebtedness has since advanced by leaps and bounds. There are now 1,000,000 Americans in France. But the Kaiser and his War-lords are still passing their victims through the fire to the Pan-German Moloch, and threatening to send German generals to teach the Austrian Army how to win offensives. It is even reported that the Germans contemplate placing the ex-king of Greece on the throne of Finland. Fantastic rumours are rife in these days; but there is only too good reason to believe the report that the ex-Tsar, the Tsaritsa, and their daughters have all been murdered by their brutal captors at Ekaterinburg. It seems but yesterday when Nicholas was acclaimed as the Saviour and regenerator of his people, and now Tsardom, irrevocably fallen from its high estate, has gone down amid scenes of butchery and barbarity that eclipse the Reign of Terror in France.

Little has happened at Westminster to indicate a consciousness on the part of the members of the great and glorious events in France. The Irish Expeditionary Force, after an absence of three months and a severe training at home, has returned to the Parliamentary Front, and their war-cry is "Devlin's the friend, not Shortt!

Above:
HUN TO HUN
Attila (to Little Willie): "Speaking as one barbarian to another, I don't recommend the neighbourhood. I found it a bit unhealthy myself."
(Attila's victorious progress across Gaol was finally checked on the plains of Châlons.)

Opposite:
VERY MUCH UP
A CHAMPAGNE COUNTER-OFFENSIVE

"But the Chief Secretary was able to make the gratifying announcement that
the voluntary recruiting campaign is to be assisted by several Nationalist M.P.'s,
including Captain Stephen Gwynn, who has been serving in the trenches, and
Colonel Lynch, who, having raised one Irish brigade to fight against us in the
Boer War, and been sentenced to death for doing it, has now, with an inconsistency we cannot too gratefully recognise, undertaken to raise another to fight on
our side. Mr. Bonar Law has revealed the interesting fact that only 288 members
of the House of Commons have received titles, decorations, or offices of profit

since it was elected in December, 1910. The unnoticed residue are probably wondering whether it is their own modesty or the shortsightedness of Ministers that has caused them to be passed over. Mr. Billing, after several pathetic but futile efforts to regain his place in the limelight, has at last succeeded in getting himself named, suspended, and forcibly assisted by four stalwart officials in his exit from the House—the most salutary movement, in the opinion of most members, with which he has yet been connected.

Admiral Sir Rosslyn Wemyss, in a recent speech, said that the association between the two Services, the Royal Navy and the Mercantile Marine, had been so close during the War, whatever that association might have been before, that it seemed to him almost incredible that it could ever be broken asunder. The First Sea Lord's statement is welcome and natural. But there is nothing really new in this solidarity of the seas. The Secret of the Ships is an old story:

> On their ventures in the service of a Tudor King or Queen
>   All the ships were just as like as they could be,
> For the merchantman gave battle, while the Royal ship was seen
>   As a not too simple trader over-sea:
> Being heirs to ancient customs, when their upper sails came down
>   As a token of respect in passing by,
> They would add the salutation in a language of their own,
>   "God speed you, we be sisters, thou and I."
>
> As the centuries receded came a parting of the ways
>   Till in time the separation went so far
> That a family was founded who were traders all their days,
>   And another who were always men-of-war;
> But whene'er they dipped their colours, one in faith, they understood—
>   And the sea, who taught them both, could tell you why—
> That the custom never altered, so the greeting still held good,
>   "God speed you, we be sisters, thou and I."
>
> Then in days of common sacrifice and peril was it strange
>   That they ratified the union of the past?
> While their Masters, unsuspecting, greatly marvelled at the change,
>   But they prayed with all their souls that it would last;
> And the ships, who know the secret, go rejoicing on their way,
>   For whatever be the ensign that they fly,
> Such as keep the seas with honour are united when they pray,
>   "God speed you, we be sisters, thou and I."

"War Pictures"

The Mother: "Of course, I don't understand them, dear; but they give me a dreadful feeling. I can't bear to look at them. Is it really like that at the Front?"

The Warrior (who has seen terrible things in battle): "Thank heaven, no, mother."

England deplores the death of Lord Rhondda, who achieved success in the most irksome and invidious of offices. He undertook the duties of Food Controller in broken health, never spared himself, and died in harness. It is to be hoped that he realised what was the truth—that he had won not only the confidence but the gratitude of the public.

Spain has rendered herself unpleasantly conspicuous by developing and exporting a new form of influenza, and a Spanish astrologer predicts the end of the world in a few months' time. But we are not going to allow those petty distractions to take our minds off the War. Here we may note that Baron Burian's recent message indicates that but for the War everything would be all right in Austria. Our artists are certainly determined not to let us forget it. But the most valuable pictures do not find their way into galleries, though they do not lack appreciative spectators.

No record of the month would be complete without notice of the unique way in which the Fourth of July has been celebrated by John Bull and Uncle Sam in France. Truly such a meeting as this does make amends.

Camouflage Officer: "That's very clever. Who did it?"
Sergeant: "Oh, that's by Perkins, sir—quite an expert. Used to paint sparrows before the war and sell 'em for canaries."

August, 1918.

July was a glorious month for the Allies, and August is even better. It began with the recovery of Soissons; a week later it was the turn of the British, and Sir Douglas Haig struck hard on the Amiens front; since then the enemy have been steadily driven back by the unrelenting pressure of the Allies, Bapaume and Noyon have been recaptured, and with their faces set for home the Germans have learnt to recognise in a new and unpleasant sense the truth of the Kaiser's saying, "The worst is behind us." The 8th of August was a bad day for Germany, for it showed that the counter-offensive was not to be confined to one section; that henceforth no respite would be allowed from hammer-blows. The German High Command endeavours to tranquillise the German people by *communiqués*, the gist of which may thus be rendered in verse:

In those very identical regions
    That sunder the Marne from the Aisne
We advanced to the rear with our legions
    Long ago and have done it again;
Fools murmur of errors committed,

But every intelligent man
Has accepted the view that we flitted
   According to plan.

The French rivers have found their voice again:

'Twas the voice of the Marne
That began it with "Garn!
Full speed, Fritz, astern!"
Then the Ourcq and the Crise
Sang "Move on, if you please."
The Ardre and the Vesle
Took up the glad tale,
And cried to the Aisne
"Wash out the Hun stain."
So all the way back from the Marne the French rivers
Have given the Boches in turn the cold shivers.

Hindenburg has confided to a newspaper correspondent that the German people need to develop the virtue of patience. According to the *Berliner Tageblatt* he has
declared that he was not in favour of the July offensive. Ludendorrf, on the other
hand, may fairly point out that it isn't his offensive any longer. Anyhow, Hindenburg
is fairly entitled to give Ludendorff the credit of it since Ludendorff's friends have
always said that he supplied the old Mud-Marshal with brains. The amenities of the
High Command are growing lively, since the Navy is also concerned, and the failure of the U-boats to check the influx of American troops needs a lot of explaining
away.

The good news from the Front has been received at home with remarkable composure, when one considers the acute anxiety of the last four months. But it is
the way of England to endure felicity with calmness and adversity with fortitude.
In the House of Lords Lord Inchcape and Lord Emmott have been propitiat-
ing Nemesis by their warnings of the gloomy financial future that is in store for
us, while in the Commons the Bolshevist group below the gangway are apparently much perturbed by the prospect that Russia may be helped on to her legs
again by the Allies. Mr. Dillon's indictment of the Government for their treatment of Ireland has had, however, a welcome if unexpected result. Mr. Shortt,
the new Chief Secretary, an avowed and unrepentant Home Ruler, has been
telling Mr. Dillon's followers a few plain truths about themselves: that they have
made no effort to turn the Home Rule Act into a practical measure; that instead
of denouncing Sinn Fein they had followed its lead; that they had attacked the
Irish executive when they ought to have supported it, and by their refusal to help

"According to Plan"
Little Willie: "Well, Father wanted a war of movement, and now he's got it!"

recruiting had forfeited the sympathy of the British working classes. Mr. Lloyd George, in his review of the War, warned the peacemongers not to expect their efforts to succeed until the enemy knew he was 'beaten, but vouchsafed no information as to his alleged intention to go to the country in the political sense. In spite of the Premier's warning the Pacificists made another futile attempt on the very next day to convince the House that the Germans were ready to make an honest peace if only our Government would listen to it. They were well answered by Mr. Robertson, who was a Pacificist himself until this War converted him, and by Mr. Balfour who declared that we were quite ready to talk to Germany as soon as she showed any sign of a change of heart. Up to the present there has been no sign of it.

Food is still the universal topic. Small green apples, says a contemporary, are proving popular. A boy correspondent, however, desires Mr. Punch to say that he has a little inside information to the contrary. Nottingham children, it is stated, are to be paid 3d. a pound for gathering blackberries, but they are not to use their own receptacles. Captain Amundsen is on his way to the Pole, but we fear that he will not find any cheese there. The vocabulary of food control has even made its way to the nursery. A small girl on being informed by her nurse that a new little baby brother had come to live with her promptly replied: "Well, he can't stay unless he's brought his coupons."

VON POT AND VON KETTLE
German General: "Why the devil don't you stop these Americans coming across? That's your job."
German Admiral: "And why the devil don't you stop 'em when they *are* across ? That's yours."

Yet one of Mr. Punch's poets, in prophetic and optimistic strain, has actually dared to speculate on the delights of life without "Dora"; Dickens, with the foresight of genius, wrote in "David Copperfield" how his hero "felt it would have been an act of perfidy to Dora to have a natural relish for my dinner."

The enterprise of *The Times* in securing the reminiscences of the Kaiser's American dentist (or gum-architect, as he is called in his native land) has aroused mingled feelings. But the Kaiser is reported to have stated in no ambiguous terms that if, after the War, any Americans are to be given access to him, from Ambassadors down-

Child (who has been made much of by father home on leave for the first time for two years): "Mummy dear. I like that man you call your husband."

wards, they must be able neither to read nor write. *The Times* is also responsible for the headline: "The Archangel Landing." There was a rumour of something of this kind after Mons, but this is apparently official.

One prominent effect of the War has been to make two Propagandist Departments flourish where none grew before, and it is to be feared that the reflection on the industry of our new officials implied in the picture on the previous page is not without foundation.

War has not only stimulated the composition, but the perusal of poetry, especially among women:

When the Armageddon diet
Makes Priscilla feel unquiet,
She prescribes herself (from Pope)
An aciduiated trope.

When the lard-hunt ruffles Rose
Wordsworth lulls her to repose,
While a snippet from the "Swan"
Stops the jam-yearn of Yvonne.

Latest addition to Ministry Staff: "What's the tea-time here?
Cicerone: "Usual—three to five-thirty."

When the man-slump makes her fretty
Susie takes to D. Rossetti,
Though her sister Arabella
Rather fancies Wilcox (Ella).

When Evangelina swoons
At the sound of the maroons,
Mrs. Hemans comes In handy
As a substitute for brandy.

And When Auntie heard by chance
That the Curate was in France,
Browning's enigmatic lyrics
Helped to save her from hysterics.

September, 1918.

Since July 15th, when the Kaiser mounted a high observation post to watch the launching of the offensive which was to achieve his crowning victory, but proved the prelude of the German collapse, the conflict has raged continuously and with uninterrupted success for the Allied Armies. The Kaiser Battle has become the Battle of Liberation. The French bore the initial burden of the attack, but since August 8 "hundreds of thousands of unbeaten Tommies," to quote the phrase of a French military expert, have entered into action in a succession of attacks started one after the other all the way up to Flanders. Rawlinson, Horne, and Byng have carried on the hammer work begun by Mangin, Gouraud, and Debeney. Péronne has been recovered, the famous Drocourt-Quéant switch-line has been breached, the Americans have flattened out the St. Mihiel salient. The perfect liaison of British and French and Americans has been a wonderful example of combined effort rendered possible by unity of command. "Marshal Foch strikes to-day at a new front," is becoming a standing head-line. And this highly desirable "epidemic of strikes" is not confined to the Western Front. As Generalissimo of all the Allied Forces the great French Marshal has planned and carried out an *ensemble* of operations designed to shatter and demoralise the enemy at every point. The long inaction on the Salonika Front has been ended by the rapid and triumphant advance of the British, French, Serbians, and Greeks under General Franchet d'Esperey. Eight days sufficed to smash the Bulgarians, and the armistice then granted was followed four days later by the surrender of Bulgaria. In less than a fort night General Allenby pushed north from Jerusalem, annihilated the Turkish armies in Palestine, and captured Damascus. And by the end of the month the Hindenburg line had been breached and gone the way of the "Wotan" line. Wotan was not a happy choice:

But even super-Germans are wont at times to nod,
And to borrow Wotan's ægis was indubitably odd;
For dark decline o'erwhelmed his line: he saw his god-head wane,
And this stately palace vanish in a red and ruinous vain.

Well may the Berlin *Tageblatt* say that "the war stares us in the face and stares very hard." When a daily paper announces "Half Crown Prince's army turned over to another General," we are curious to know how much the Half Crown Prince thinks the German Sovereign worth. But the end is not yet. Our pride in the achievements of our Armies and Generals, in the heroism of our Allies and the strategy of Marshal Foch does not blind us to the skill and tenacity with which the Germans are conducting their retreat. Fritz is a tough fighter; if only he had fought a clean fight we could look forward to a thorough reconciliation. But that is a far cry for those who have been in the war, farthest of all for our sailormen, who can never forget certain acts of frightfulness.

Hans Dans an' me was shipmates once, an' if 'e'd fought us clean,
Why shipmates still when war was done might Hans an' me 'ave been;
The truest pals a man can have are them 'e's fought before,
But—never no more, Hans Dans, my lad, so 'elp me, never no more!

Austria has issued a Peace Note, and the German Chancellor has declared that Germany is opposed to annexation in any form. The German Eagle, making it virtue of necessity, is ready to give the bird of Peace an innings.

The two Emmas, Ack and Pip, are naturally furious at the adoption of the twenty-four hours' system of reckoning time, which means that their occupation will be gone, and that like other old soldiers they will fade away. Amongst other innovations we have to note the spread of "bobbing," the further possibilities of which are alarming to contemplate.

Ferdinand, Tsar of Bulgaria, great grandson of Philippe Egalité, finding Sofia unhealthy, has been recuperating at Vienna. His future plans are vague, but it is thought he may join the ex-Kings' Club in Switzerland. Lenin, the Bolshevist Dictator, has recently experienced an attempt on his life, and retaliated in a fashion which would have done credit to a mediæval despot. England still refuses to indulge in joy bells or bunting, but the London police have seized the occasion to strike on the home front. Their operations have been promptly, if inconsistently rewarded by the removal of their chief and his elevation to the baronetcy.

Parliament is not sitting, and the voice of the Pro-Boche and the Pro-Bolsh is temporarily hushed. We have to note, however, a most welcome *rapprochement* between

STORM DRIVEN
The Kaiser: "I don't like this wind, my son. Which way is it?"
The crown Prince: "Up!"

IN RESERVE

German eagle (to German Dove): "Here, carry on for a bit, will you? I'm feeling rather run down."

ALARMING SPREAD OF BOBBING

Downing and Carmelite Streets—the *Daily Mail* has praised the Foreign Office for an "excellent piece of work," and the scapegoat, unexpectedly caressed, is sitting up and taking nourishment.

The harvest has been a success, thanks to the energy of the new land-workers, the armies behind the army:

> All the talent is here—all the great and the lesser,
>   The proud and the humble, the stout and the slim,
> The second form boy and the aged professor,
>   Grade three and the hero in want of a limb.

Four years of war have brought curious changes to "our village":

> Our baker's in the Flying Corps,
>   Our butcher's in the Buffs,
> Our one policeman cares no more
>   For running in the roughs,
> But carves a pathway to the stars
> As trooper in the Tenth Hussars.

> The Mayor's a Dublin Fusilier,
>   The clerk's a Royal Scot,
> The bellman is a brigadier
>   And something of a pot;
> The barber, though at large, is spurned;
> The Blue Boar's waiter is interned.

> The postman, now in Egypt, wears
>   A medal on his coat;
> The vet. is breeding Belgian hares,
>   The vicar keeps a goat;
> The schoolma'am knits upon her stool;
> The village idiot gathers wool.

The husbandman and his new help have undergone mutual transformation. And our cadet battalions are making them selves very much at home at Oxford and Cambridge.

The Navy still remains the silent Service, but, as the need for reticence is being relaxed by the triumph of our arms, we are beginning to learn something, though unofficially as yet, of that "plaything of the Navy and nightmare of the Huns"— the Q-boat:

First week

Second week

Third week

Fourth week

THE FARMER AND THE FARM LABOURER

She can weave a web of magic for the unsuspecting foe,
    She can scent the breath of Kultur leagues away,
She can hear a U-boat thinking in Atlantic depths below
    And disintegrate it with a Martian ray;
                She can feel her way by night
                Through the minefield of the Bight;
    She has all the tricks of science, grave and gay.

In the twinkle of a searchlight she can suffer a sea-change
    From a collier to a *Shamrock* under sail,
From a Hyper-super-Dreadnought, old Leviathan at range,
    To a lightship or a whaler or a whale;
                With some canvas and a spar
                She can mock the morning star
    As a haystack or the flotsam of a gale.

She's the derelict you chartered north of Flores outward-bound,
    She's the iceberg that you sighted coming back,
She's the salt-rimed Biscay trawler heeling home to Plymouth Sound,
    She's the phantom-ship that crossed the moon-beams' track;
                She's the rock where none should be
                In the Adriatic Sea,
    She's the wisp of fog that haunts the Skagerrack.

Recognition of services faithfully done is an endless task; but Mr. Punch is glad to print the valedictory tribute of one of the boys in blue to a V.A.D.—a class that has come in for much undeserved criticism,

While willy-nilly I must go
    A-hunting of the Hun,
You'll carry on—which now I know
(Although I've helped to rag you so)
    Means great work greatly done.

Among the minor events of the month has been the christening of a baby by the names of Grierson Plumer Haig French Smith-Dorrien, as its father served under these generals. The idea is, no doubt, to prevent the child when older from asking: "What did you do in the Great War, Daddy?"

England, as we have already said, endures its triumphs with composure. But our printers are not altogether immune from excitement. An evening paper informs us that "the dwifficuplties of passing from rigid trench warfare to field warfare are gigantic and

Cadet: "Really, from the way these College Authorities make themselves at home you'd think the place belonged to them."

perhaps unsurmountable." And only our innate sense of comradeship deters us from naming the distinguished contemporary which recently published an article entitled:

"The Importance of Bray."

October, 1918.

The growing *crescendo* of success has reached its climax in this, the most wonderful month of our *annus mirabilis*. Every day brings tidings of a new victory. St. Quentin, Cambrai, and Laon had all been recaptured in the first fortnight. On the 17th Ostend, Lille, and Douai were regained, Bruges was reoccupied on the 19th and by the 20th the Belgian Army under King Albert, reinforced by the French and Americans, and with the Second British Army under General Plumer on the right, had compelled the Germans to evacuate the whole coast of Flanders. The Battle of Liberation, which began on the Marne in July, is now waged uninterruptedly from the Meuse to the sea. Only in Lorraine has the advance of the American Army been held up by the difficulties of the *terrain* and the exceptionally stubborn resistance of the Germans.

Elsewhere the "war of movement" has gone on with un relenting energy according to Foch's plan, which suggests a revision of Pope:

Great Foch's law is by this rule exprest,
Prevent the coming, speed the parting pest.

The German, true to his character of the world's worst loser and winner, leaves behind him all manner of booby-traps, some puerile, many diabolical, which give our sappers plenty of work, cause a good many casualties, and only confirm the resolve of the victors.

According to a German paper—the *Rhenish Westphalian Gazette*—ex-criminals are being drafted into the German Army. But the Allies propose to treat them without invidious distinction. The Crown Prince recently observed that he had "many friends in the Entente countries"; as a matter of fact, we seem to be getting them at the rate of about twenty-five thousand a week. The criminals in the German Navy have again been busy, adding to their previous exploits the sinking of the passenger steamer *Leinster*, in the Irish Channel, with heavy loss of life, the worst disaster of the kind since the torpedoing of the *Lusitania*. Yet it is Germany that is the sinking ship. Ferdinand of Bulgaria has joined the League of Abdication, and according to a Sofia telegram, will devote himself to scientific pursuits. His only regret is that the Allies thought of it first. Prince Friedrich Karl of Hesse says that his accession to the throne of Finland will not take place for two years, and for the first time since his emergence into publicity we find ourselves in agreement with this monarch elect. Ludendorff has resigned. Austria is suing for peace; Count Tisza asks "Why not admit frankly that we have lost the War?" The Italians have crossed the Piave, and the Serbians have reached the Danube. Turkey has been granted an armistice, and with the daily victories of the Allies comes the daily report that the Kaiser has abdicated.

Prince Max of Baden, the successor of Hertling in the Chancellorship, whose appointment hardly bears out the promise of popular government, has issued a pacific Manifesto which inspires an "Epitaph in anticipation":

In memory of poor Prince Max,
Who, posing as the friend of Pax,
Yet was not noticeably lax
In the true Teuton faith which hacks
Its way along forbidden tracks,
Marks bloody dates on almanacs
And holds all promises as wax;
Breeding, where once we knew Hans Sachs,
A race of monomaniacs ...

SOLDIER AND CIVILIAN

Marshal Foch (to Messrs. Clemenceau, Wilson and Lloyd George): "If you're going up that road, gentlemen, look out for booby-traps,"

But now illusion's mirror cracks,
The radiant vision fades, the axe
Lies at the root. So farewell, Max!

Certain people have proclaimed their opinion that the German nation ought not to be humiliated. When all is said, Mr. Punch saves his pity for our murdered dead.

Parliament has met again, not that there is any very urgent need for their labours just now. With a caution that seemed excessive Mr. Bonar Law has thought it premature to discuss a military situation changing every hour—though happily always for the better—or even to propose a formal Vote of Thanks to men who are daily adding to their harvest of laurels. On better grounds discussion of Mr. Wilson's famous "fourteen points" and of demobilisation has been deprecated. The suggestion—made opportunely on Trafalgar Day—for securing marks of distinction for our merchant seamen gained a sympathetic hearing, and the proposal to make women eligible for Parliament has been carried after a serious debate by an overwhelming majority in which the *ci-devant* anti-suffragists were as prominent as the others. Five years ago such a motion would have furnished an orgy of alleged humour, and been laughed out of the House. Mr. Dillon and his colleagues have put a great many questions about the torpedoing of the *Leinster* and the lack of an escort. But it is unfortunate that their tone suggested more indignation with the alleged laches of the Admiralty than horror at the German crime. Irish indignation over the outrage, according to a Nationalist M.P., is intense; but not to the point of expressing itself in khaki.

The woes of the Irish harvest labourers in England have not yet been fully appreciated, and seem to demand a revised version of "Moira O'Neill's" beautiful poem:

The Irish Exile

Over here in England I'm slavin' in the rain;
Six-an-Six a day we get, an' beds that wanst were clane;
Weary on the English work, 'tis killin me that same—
Och, Muckish Mountain, where I used to lie an' dhrame!

At night the windows here are black as Father Murphy's hat;
'Tis fivepence for a pint av beer, an' thin ye can't get that;
Their beef has shtrings like anny harp, for dacent ham I hunt—
Och, Muckish Mountain, an' my pig's sweet grunt!

Sure there's not a taste av butthermilk that wan can buy or beg,
Thin their sweet milk has no crame, an' is as blue as a duck-egg;

DIE NACHT AM RHEIN

PROSPEROUS IRISH FARMER: "And what about the War, your Riverence? Do ye think it will hould?"

Their whisky is as wake as wather-gruel in a howl—
Och, Muckish Mountain, where the *poteen* warms yer sowl!

'Tis mesilf that longs for Irish air an' gran' ould Donegal,
Where there's lashins and there's lavins and no scarcity at all;
Where no wan cares about the War, but just to ate an' play—
Och, Muckish Mountain, wid yer feet beside the say!

Sure these Englishmin don't spare thimselves in this thremenjus fight;
They say 'tis life or death for thim, an', faith, they may be right;
But Father Murphy tells me that it's no consarn av mine—
Och, Muckish Mountain, where the white clouds shine!

Over there in Ireland we're very fond av peace,
Though we break the heads av Orangentin an' batther the police;
For we're a agin the Gosrernmint wheriver we may be—
Och, Muckish Mountain, an' the wild wind blowin' free!

If they tuk me out to Flandhers, bedad I'd have to fight,
An' I'm tould thim Jarman vagabones won't let ye sleep at night;
So I'm going home to Ireland wid English notes galore—
Och, Muckish Mountain, I will niver lave ye more!

By way of contrast there is the mood of the Old Contemptibles, but it is only fair to add that there are Irishmen among them:

The Old-Timer

'E ain't bin 'ung with medals, Like a lot o' chaps abaht;
'E's wore a little dingy but 'e isn't wearin' aht;
'Is ole tin 'at is battered, but it isn't battered in,
An' if 'e ain't fergot to grouse, 'e ain't fergot to grin.

I fancy that 'e's aged a bit since fust the War begun;
'E's 'ad 'is fill o' figihtin' an' 'e's 'ad 'is share o' fun;
'Is eyes is kind o' quiet an' 'is mouth is sort o' set,
But if I didn't know 'im well I wouldn't know 'im yet.

I recollec' the look of 'im the time o' the retreat,
The blood was through 'is toonic an' the skin was off 'is feet;
But "Come aboard the bus," say 'e, "or you'll be lef' be'ind!"
An' takes me weight upon 'is back—it 'asn't slip me mind.

It might 'ave 'appened yesterday, it comes to me so plain;
'E's dahn an' up a dozen t a-reeling through the rain;
It might 'ave bin lars' Saturday I seem to 'ear 'im say:
"There's plenty room a-top, me lad, an' nothin' more to pay."

'E ain't bin 'ung with medals like a blackamore with beads;
'E doesn't figure on the screen a-doin' darin' deeds;
But reckon I'll be lucky if I gets to Kingdom Come
Along o' that Contemptible wot wouldn't leave a chum.

Amongst other items of news we have to chronicle the appointment of Mr. Arnold Bennett as a Director of Propaganda, the steady growth of goat-keeping, and the exactions of taxi-drivers. It is now suggested that if one of these pirates should charge you largely in excess of his legal fare, you should tell him that you have nothing less than a five-pound note. If you have an honest face and speak kindly he will probably accept the amount.

First contemptible: "D'you remember halting here on the retreat, George?"
Second Ditto: "Can't call it to mind, somehow. Was it that little village in the wood there down by the river, or was it that place with the cathedral and allthem factories?"

Mr. Bonar Law has been making trips to and from France by aeroplane. The report that a number of members of the Opposition have been invited by the Admiralty to make a descent in a depth-charge turns out to be unfounded. The prospects of peace are being discussed on public platforms, but, as yet, with commendable discretion. Mr. Roberts, our excellent Minister of Labour, has made bold to say that "the happenings of the last six weeks justify us in the belief that peace is much nearer than it was during the earlier part of the year." And a weekly paper has offered a prize of £500 to the reader who predicts the date when the War will end. Meanwhile, Hanover is said to have made Hindenburg a birthday present of a house in the neighbourhood of the Zoological Gardens in that city, and we suggest that before this gift is incorporated in the peace-terms the words "the neighbourhood of" should be deleted.

November, 1918.

The end has come with a swiftness that has outdone the hopes of the most sanguine optimists. In the first eleven days of November we have seen history in the making on a larger scale and with larger possibilities than at any time since the age of Napoleon, perhaps since the world began.

THE SANDS RUN OUT

Victory!

To take the chief events in order, the Versailles Conference opened on the 1st; on the 3rd Austria gave in and the resolve of the German Naval High Command to challenge the Grand Fleet in the North Sea was paralysed by the mutiny at Kiel; on the 5th the Versailles Conference gave full powers to Marshal Foch to arrange the terms of an armistice, and President Wilson addressed the last of his Notes to Germany; on the 6th the American Army reached Sedan; on the 9 Marshal Foch received Erzberger and the other German Envoys, the Berlin Revolution broke out, and the Kaiser abdicated; on the 10th the Kaiser fled to Holland, and the British reached Mons. The wheel had come full circle. The Belgian, British, French, and American Armies now formed a semi-circle from Ghent to Sedan, and threatened to surround the German Armies already in retreat and crowded into the narrow valley of the Meuse. Everything was ready for Foch's final attack; indeed, he was on the point of attacking when the Germans, recognising that they were faced with the prospect of a Sedan ten times greater than that of 1870 signed on November 11 an armistice which was equivalent to a military capitulation, and gave Marshal Foch all that he wanted without the heavy losses which further fighting would have undoubtedly involved. He had shown himself the greatest military genius of the War. Here, in the words of one of his former colleagues at the Ecole de Guerre, he proved himself free from the stains which have so often tarnished great leaders in war, the lust of conquest and personal ambition. Not only the Allies, but the whole world owes an incalculable debt to this soldier of justice, compact of reason and faith, imperturbable in adversity, self-effacing in the hour of victory. Glorious also is the record of the other French Generals: the strong-souled Pétain, hero of Verdun; the heroic Maunoury; Castlenau and Mangin, Gouraud, Debeney, and Franchet d'Esperey, Captains Courageous, worthy of France, her cause, and her indomitable *poilus*. In the record of acknowledgment France stands first since her sacrifices and losses have been heaviest, and she gave us in Foch the chief organiser of victory, in Clemenceau the most inspiring example of in trepid statesmanship. But the War could not have been won without England and the Empire; without the ceaseless vigil in the North Sea; without the heroes of Jutland and Coronel, of the Falkland Isles and Zeebrugge, of the Fleets behind the Fleet; without the services of Smith at Mons, French at Ypres; without the dogged endurance, the inflexible will and the self-sacrificing loyalty of Haig; the dash of Maude and Allenby; the steadfast leadership in defence and offence of Plumer and Byng, Home and Rawlinson and Birdwood.

These are only some of the heroes who have added to the glories of our blood and State, but the roll is endless—wonderful gunners and sappers and airmen and dispatch riders, devoted surgeons and heroic nurses, stretcher-bearers and ambulance drivers. But Mr. Punch's special heroes are the Second Lieutenants and the Tommy who went on winning the War all the time and never said that he was winning it until it was won.

OUR MAN
With Mr. Punch's Grateful compliments to Field-Marshal Sir Douglas Haig.

As for the young officers, dead and living, their record is the best answer to the critics, mostly of the arm-chair type, who have chosen this time to assail our public school system. In the papers of one of them killed on August 28 there was found an article written in reply to "The Loom of Youth," ending with these words: "Perhaps the greatest consolation of these attacks on our greatest heritage in England (for we are the unique possessors of the Public Schools) is the conviction that they will have but little effect. Every public school boy is serving, and one in every six gives up his life. They cannot be such bad places after all."

Of the great mistakes made by Germany perhaps the greatest was in reckoning on the detachment of the Dominions. The Canadians have made answer on a hundred stricken fields before and after Vimy Ridge. Australia gave her goodliest at Gallipoli, crowning the imperishable glory of those who died there by her refusal to make a grievance of the apparent failure of the expedition, and by the amazing achievement of her troops in the last six months of the War.

The immortal dead, British, Australians, New Zealanders, who fell in the great adventure of the narrow straits are not forgotten in the hour of triumph.

Gallipoli

Qui procul hinc ante diem perierunt.

Ye unforgotten, that for a great dream died,
    Whose failing sense darkened on peaks unwon,
Whose souls went forth upon the wine-dark tide
            To seas beyond the sun,
Far off, far off, but ours and England's yet,
Know she has conquered! Live again, and let
    The clamouring trumpets break oblivion!

Not as we dreamed, nor as you strove to do,
    The strait is cloven, the crag is made our own;
The salt grey herbs have withered over you,
            The stars of Spring gone down,
And your long loneliness has lain unstirred
By touch of home, unless some migrant bird
    Flashed eastward from the white cliffs to the brown.

Hard by the nameless dust of Argive men,
    Remembered and remote, like theirs of Troy,
Your sleep has been, nor can ye wake again
            To any cry of joy;

THE FINAL

Tommy (ex-footballer): "We was just wipin' them off the face of the earth when Foch blows his whistle and shouts 'Temps!'"

Summers and snows have melted on the waves,
And past the noble silence of your graves
　　The merging waters narrow and deploy.

But not in vain, not all in vain, thank God;
　　All that you were and all you m have been
Was given to the cold effacing sod,
　　　　　Unstrewn with garlands green;
The valour and the vision that were yours
Lie not with broken spears and fallen towers,
　　With glories perishable of all things seen.

Children of one dear land and every sea,
　　At last fulfilment comes—the night is o'er;
Now, as at Samothrace, swift Victory
　　　　Walks winged on the shore;
And England, deathless Mother of the dead,
Gathers, with lifted eyes and unbowed head,
　　Her silent sons into her arms once more.

Crowns and thrones have rocked and toppled of late, but our King and Queen, by their unsparing and unfaltering devotion to duty, by their simplicity of life and unerring instinct for saying and doing the right thing, have not only set a fine example, but strengthened their hold on the loyalty of all classes. And King Albert, who defied Germany at the outset, shared the dangers of his soldiers in retreat and disaster, and throughout the war proved an inspiration to his people, has been spared to lead them to victory and has gloriously come into his own again. His decision to resist Germany was perhaps the most heroic act of the War, and he has emerged from his tremendous ordeal with world-wide prestige and unabated distaste for the limelight. The liberation and resurrection of Belgium and Serbia have been two of the most splendid outcomes of the World War, as the *débâcle* in Russia and the martyrdom of Armenia have been its greatest tragedies.

Parliament has been seen at its best and worst. When the Prime Minister rose in the House on the afternoon of the 11th to announce the terms of the Armistice signed at 5 a.m. that morning, members from nearly all parts of the House rose to acclaim him. Even "the ranks of Tuscany" on the front Opposition bench joined in the general cheering. Only Mr. Dillon and his half-dozen supporters remained moody and silent, and when Mr. Speaker, in his gold-embroidered joy-robes, headed a great procession to St. Margaret's Church, and the ex-Premier and his successor—the man who drew the sword of Britain in the war for freedom and the man whose good fortune it has been to replace it in the sheath—fell in side by side, behind them walked the representatives of every party save one. Mr. Dillon and his associates had more urgent business in one of the side lobbies—to consider, perhaps, why Lord Grey of Falloden, in his eve-of-war speech, had referred to Ireland as "the one bright spot." This Irish aloofness is wondrously illustrated by the *Sunday Independent* of Dublin, which, in its issue of November 10, spoke of a racing event as the only redeeming feature of "an unutterably dull week." We have to thank Mr. Dillon, however, for unintentionally enlivening the dulness of the discussion on the relations of Lord Northcliffe to the Ministry of Information and his forecast of the peace terms. Mr. Baldwin, for the Government, while endeavouring to allay the curiosity of members, said that "Napoleons will be Napoleons." Mr. Dillon seemed to desire the appointment of a "Northcliffe Controller," but that is impracticable. All our bravest men are too busy to take on the job. Better still was the pointed query of Lord Henry Bentinck, "Is it not possible to take Lord Northcliffe a little too seriously?" But there are other problems to which the House has been addressing itself with a justifiable seriousness— "Dora" and demobilisation, the shortage of food and coal, and the question how at the same time we are to provide for the outlay of coals of fire and feed the Huns and not the guns.

And how has England taken the news? In the main soberly and in a spirit of infinite thankfulness, though in too many thousands of homes the loss of our splendid, noble and gallant sons—alas! so often only sons—who made victory possible by the gift of their lives, has made rejoicing impossible for those who are left to mourn them. Yet there is consolation in the knowledge that if they had lived to extreme old age they could never have made a nobler thing of their lives. Shakespeare, who "has always been there before," wrote the epitaph of those who fell in France when he spoke of one who gave

> His body to that pleasant country's earth,
> And his pure soul unto his captain, Christ,
> Under whose colours he had fought so long.

And it is a source of unspeakable joy that our children are safe. For though to most of them their ignorance has been bliss, they have not escaped the horrors of a war in which non-combatants have suffered worse than ever before. Only the healing hand of time can allay the grief of those for whom there can be no reunion on earth with their nearest and dearest:

> At last the dawn creeps in with golden fingers
> Seeking my eyes, to bid them open wide
> Upon a world at peace, where Sweetness lingers,
> Where Terror is at rest and Hate has died.

ARMISTICE DAY

Small Child (excitedly): "Oh, Mother, what *do* you think? They've given us a whole holiday to-day in aid of the war."

Loud soon shall sound a pæan of thanksgiving
  From happy women, welcoming their men,
Life born anew of joy to see them living.
  Mother of Pity, what shall I do then?

Of the people at large Mr. Punch cannot better the praise of one, the late Mr. Henry James, who was nothing if not critical, and who proved his love of England by adopting her citizenship in the darkest hour of her need: "They were about as good, above all, when it came to the stress, as could well be expected of people. They didn't know how good they were," and if they lacked imagination they stimulated it immensely in others.

Apart from some effervescence in the great cities, Armistice Day was celebrated without exultation or extravagance. In one village that we know of the church bells were rung by women. In London our deliverance was to many people marked in the most dramatic way by the breaking of his long silence by Big Ben:

Gone are the days when sleep alone could break
  War's grim and tyrannous spells;
Now it is rest and joy to lie awake
  And listen to the bells.

IN HONOUR OF THE BRITISH NAVY
To commemorate the surrender of the German Fleet

So the Great War ended. But there yet remained the most dramatic episode of all—the surrender of the German Fleet to Admiral Beatty at Scapa Flow—a surrender unprecedented in naval history, a great victory won without striking a blow, which yet brought no joy to our Grand Fleet. For our admirals and captains and bluejackets felt that the Germans had smirched the glory of the fighting men of the sea, hitherto maintained in untarnished splendour by all vanquished captains from the days of Carthage to those of Cervera and Cradock.

Epilogue

It remains to trace in brief retrospect the record of "the months between"—a period of test and trial almost as severe as that of the War.

Having steadfastly declined the solution of a Peace without Victory, the Allies entered last November on the transitional period of Victory without Peace. The fighting was ended in the main theatres of war, the Kaiser and Crown Prince, discrowned and discredited, had sought refuge in exile, the great German War machine had been smashed, and demobilisation began at a rate which led to inevitable congestion and disappointment. The prosaic village blacksmith was not far out when, in reply to the vicar's pious hope that the time had come to beat our sword into a ploughshare, he observed, "Well, I don't know, sir. Speaking as a blacksmith of forty-five years' experience, I may tell you it can't be done." "The whole position is provisional," said the *Times* at the end of November. If Germany Austria, and Russia were to be fed, how was it to be done without disregarding the prior claims of Serbia and Roumania? Even at home the food question still continued to agitate the public mind.

The General Election of December, 1918, which followed the dissolution of the longest Parliament since the days of Charles II, was a striking, if temporary proof, of the persistence of the rationing principle. It proved a triumph for the Coalition "Coupon" and for Mr. Lloyd George; the extremists and Pacificists were snowed under; Mr. Asquith was rejected and his followers reduced to a mere handful; Labour came back with an increased representation, though not as great as it desired or deserved. The triumph of the irreconcilables in Ireland was a foregone but sinister conclusion to their activities in the War, and an ominous prelude to their subsequent efforts to wreck the Peace. The pledges in regard to indemnities, the treatment of the Kaiser, and conscription so lavishly given by the Coalition Leaders caused no little misgiving at the time, and pledges, like curses, have an awkward way of coming home to roost. Mr. Punch's views on the Kaiser, expressed in his Christmas Epilogue, are worth recalling. Mr. Punch did not clamour for the death penalty, or wish to hand him over to the tender mercies of German Kultur. "The only fault he committed in German eyes is that he lost the War, and I wouldn't have him punished for the wrong offence—for some thing, indeed, which was our doing as much

"Don't you think we ought to hang the Kaiser. Mrs. 'Arris?"
"It ain't the Kaiser I'm worrying about—it's the bloke what interjuiced this war-bacon."

as his. No, I think I would just put him out of the way of doing further harm, in some distant penitentiary like the Devil's Island, and leave him to himself to think it all over; as *Caponsacchi* said of *Guido* in ' The Ring and the Book':

> Not to die so much as slide out of life,
> Pushed by the general horror and common hate
> Low, lower—left o' the very edge of things."

Christmas, 1918, was more than "the Children's Truce." Our bugles had "sung truce," the war cloud had lifted, the invaded sky was once more free of "the grim geometry of Mars," and though very few households could celebrate the greatest of anniversaries with unbroken ranks, the mercy of reunion was granted to many homes. Yet Mr. Punch, in his Christmas musings on the solemn memory of the dead who gave us this hour, could not but realise the greatness of the task that lay before

REUNITED
Strasbourg, December 8th, 1918.

RECONSTRUCTION: A NEW YEAR'S TASK

us if we were to make our country worthy of the men who fought and died for her. The War was over, but another had yet to be waged against poverty and sordid environment; against the disabilities of birth; against the abuse of wealth; against the mutual suspicions of Capital and Labour; against sloth, indifference, self-complacency, and short memories.

So the Old Year passed, the last of a terrible *quinquennium*, bringing grounds for thankfulness and hope along with the promise of unrest and upheaval: with Alsace-Lorraine reunited to France, with the British army holding its Watch on the Rhine, and with all eyes fixed on Paris, the scene of the Peace Conference, already invaded by an international army of delegates, experts, advisers, secretaries, typists, 500 American journalists, and President Wilson.

Great Expectations and their Tardy Fulfilment, thus in headline fashion might one summarise the story of 1919, with Peace, the world's desire, waiting for months outside the door of the Conference Chamber, with civil war in Germany, Berlin bombed by German airmen, and anarchy in Russia, and here at home impatience and discomfort, aggravated in the earlier months by strikes and influenza, the largely increased numbers of unemployed politicians, the weariest and dreariest of winter weather.

Yet even January had its alleviations in the return of the banana, the prospect of unlimited lard, a distinct improvement in the manners of the retail tradesman, the typographical fireworks of the *Times* in honour of President Wilson, and the retreat of Lord Northcliffe to the sunny south. Lovers of sensation were conciliated by the appointment of "F.E." to the Lord Chancellorship, the outbreak of Jazz, and the discovery of a French author that the plays usually attributed to Shakespeare were written by Lord Derby, though not apparently the present holder of the title. The loss, through rejection or withdrawal, of so many of his old Parliamentary puppets was a serious blow to Mr. Punch, but the old Liberals, buried like the Babes in the Wood beneath a shower of Coalition coupons, already showed a sanguine spirit, and the departure of the freaks could be contemplated with resignation. The great Exodus to Paris began in December, but it reached its height in January. The mystery of the Foreign Office official who had *not* gone was cleared up by the discovery that he was the caretaker, a pivotal man who could not be demobilised. Another exodus of a less desirable sort was that of the Sinn Fein prisoners, which gave rise to the rumour that the Lord Lieutenant had threatened that if they destroyed any more jails they would be rigorously released. Sinn Fein, which refused to fight Germany, had already begun to play at a new sort of war. Australia was preparing to welcome the homing transports sped with messages of Godspeed from the Motherland:

Rich reward your hearts shall hold,
　None less dear if long delayed,
For with gifts of wattle-gold

Shall your country's debt be paid;
From her sunlight's golden store
She shall heal your hurt of war.

Ere the mantling Channel's mist
    Dim your distant decks and spars,
And your flag that victory kissed
    And Valhalla hung with stars—
Crowd and watch our signal fly:
    "Gallant hearts, good-bye! *Good-bye!* "

February, a month of comparative anti-climax, witnessed the reassembling of
Parliament, fuller than ever of members if not of wisdom. As none of the Sinn Feiners
were present, nor indeed any representative of Irish Nationalism, the proceedings were
as orderly as a Quaker's funeral, save for the arrival of one member on a motor-scooter.
Perhaps the most interesting information elicited during the debates was this—that
every question put down costs the tax-payer a guinea. On February 20th there were
282 on the Order Paper, and Mr. Punch was moved to wonder whether this cascade of
curiosity might be abated if every questionist were obliged to contribute half the cost,
the amount to be deducted from his official salary. The Speaker, the greatest of living
Parliamentarians, was re-elected by acclamation. Though human and humorous, he
has grown into something almost more like an institution than a man, like Big Ben,
that great patriot and public servant who never struck during the war, The best news in
February was that of M. Clemenceau's escape, though wounded, from the Anarchist
assassin who had attempted to translate Trotsky's threat into action. But it did not help
on the proposed Conference with the Russians at Prinkipo or encourage the prospect
of any tangible results from the deliberation of the Prinkipotentiaries. The plain man
could see no third choice beyond supporting Bolshevism or anti-Bolshevism. But
according to our Prime Minister, we were committed to a compromise. The Allies
were not prepared to intervene in force, and they could not leave Russia to stew in
her own hell-broth. Meanwhile the chief criminal, Germany, had begun to utter *ad
misericordiam* appeals for the relaxation of the Armistice terms on the score of their
cruelty; and Count Brockdorff-Rantzau gave us a foretaste of his quality by declaring
that "Germany cannot be treated as a second-rate nation."

At home, though the rays of "sweet unrationed revelry" were still to come, and
Dulce Domum could not yet be sung in every sense, February brought us some
relief in the demobilisation of the pivotal pig. And the decision to hold a National
Industrial Conference was of encouraging augury for the settlement of industrial
strife on the basis of a full inquiry and frank statement of facts. In other walks of life
reticence still has its charms, and even in February people had begun to ask who the
General was who had threatened not to write a book about the War.

THE 1919 MODEL
Mr. Punch: "They've given you a fine new machine, Mr. Premier, and you've got plenty of spirit, but look out for bumps."

"How was it you never let your mother know you'd won the V.C. ?"
"It wasna ma turn tae write."

ENGLAND EXPECTS
(With Mr. Punch's best hopes for the success of the National Industrial Conference.)
Both Lions (together): "Unaccustomed as I am to lie down with anything but a lamb, still, for the sake of the public good ..."

March, the mad month, remained true to type. Even Mr. Punch found it hard to preserve his equanimity:

O Month, before your final moon is set
   Much may have happened—anything, in fact;
More than in any March that I have met
   (Last year excepted) fearful nerves are racked;
Anarchy does with Russia what it likes;
   Paris is put conundrums very knotty;
And here in England, with its talk of strikes,
   Men, like your own March hares, seem going dotty.

Abroad the ex-Kaiser was very busy sawing trees, possibly owing to an hallucination that they were German Generals.

At home the Government decided to release such of the Sinn Fein prisoners as had not already saved them the trouble, and a Coal Industry Commission was appointed on which no representative of the general public was invited to sit—that is to say, the patient, much enduring consumer, not the public which has all along sought to discount peace by premature whooping, jubilating, and Jazzing. For the Dove of Peace, though in strict training, seemed in danger of collapsing under the weight of the League of Nations' olive bough, to say nothing of other perils, notably the Bolshy-bird, a most obscene brand of vulture.

Mr. Wilson was once more on the Atlantic, and Mr. Lloyd George, distracted between his duties in Paris and the demands of Labour, recalled Sir Boyle Roche's bird, or the circus performer riding two horses at once. In Parliament the interpretation of election pledges occupied a good deal of time, and Mr. Bonar Law twice declared the policy of the Government in regard to indemnities as being to demand the largest amount that Germany could pay, but not to demand what we knew she couldn't pay. It would have saved him a great deal of trouble if at the General Election the Government spokesmen had insisted as much upon the second half of the policy as they did on the first. Earnest appeals for economy were made from the Treasury Bench on the occasion of the debate on the Civil Service Estimates, now swollen to five times their pre-war magnitude, and were heartily applauded by the House. To show how thoroughly they had gone home, Mr. Adamson, the Labour Leader, immediately pressed for an increase in the salaries of Members of Parliament.

On the Rhine the efforts of our army of occupation to present the stern and forbidding air supposed to mark our dealings with the inhabitants were proving a lamentable failure. You can't produce a really good imitation of a Hun without lots of practice. Gloating is entirely foreign to the nature of Thomas Atkins, and he could not pass a child yelling in the gutter without stooping to comfort it. At home

THE EASTER OFFERING

Mr. Lloyd George (fresh from Paris): "I don't say it's a perfect egg, but parts of it, as the saying is, are excellent."

OVERWEIGHTED

President Wilson: "Here's your olive branch. Now get busy."

Dove of peace: "Of course, I want to please everybody, but isn't this a bit thick?"

his education was proceeding on different lines. The period of reaction had set in, and unwonted exertions were necessary to stimulate his interest. Such artless devices were, however, preferable to the pastime, already fashionable in more exalted circles, of kicking a total stranger round the room to the accompaniment of cymbals, a motor siren, and a frying pan.

After a month of madness it was not to be wondered at that we should have a month of muzzling, though the enforcement of the order might have been profit-

HOW TO BRIGHTEN THE PERIOD OF REACTION
Mother (to son who has fought on most of the Fronts): "Don't you know what to do with
yourself, George? Why don't you 'ave a walk down the road, dear?"
Father: "Ah, 'e ain't seen the corner where they pulled down Simmondses' fish-shop 'as 'e, Ma?"

ably extended from dogs to journalists. The secrecy maintained by the Big Four—a
phrase invented by America—the conflict of the idealists with the realists, and the
temporary break-away of the Italian wrestler, Orlando, were bound to excite comment. But a shattered world could not be rebuilt in a day, with Bolshevist wolves
prowling about the Temple of Peace, and the Dove at sea between the Ark and
Archangel. The Covenant of the League of Nations, though in a diluted form, had
at last taken shape, the Peace Machine had got a move on, and the Premier's spirited,
if not very dignified, retaliation on the newspaper snipers led to an abatement of
unnecessary hostilities, though the pastime of shooting policemen with comparative
impunity still flourished in Ireland, and the numbers and cost of our "army of inoc-
cupation" still continued to increase. Innumerable queries were made in Parliament
on the subject of the unemployment dole, but the announcement that the Admiralty
did not propose to perpetuate the title "Grand Fleet" for the principal squadron of
His Majesty's Navy passed without comment. The Grand Fleet is now a part of the
History that it did so much to make.

"END OF A PERFECT 'TAG'"

GHOSTS AT VERSAILLES

May and June were "hectic" months, in which the reaction from the fatigues and restraints of War found vent in an increased disinclination for work, encouraged by a tropical sun. These were the months of the resumption of cricket, the Victory Derby, the flood of honours, and the flying of the Atlantic, with a greater display of popular enthusiasm over the gallant airmen who failed in that feat than over the generals who had won the War. They were also the months of the duel between Mr. Smillie and the Dukes, the discovery of oil in Derbyshire, the privileged excursion into War polemics of Lord French, unrest in Egypt, renewed trouble with the police, and a shortage of beer, boots and clothes.

But though the Big Four had been temporarily reduced to a Big Three by Italy's withdrawal, and though M. Clemenceau, Mr. Lloyd George, and President Wilson had all suffered in prestige by the slow progress of the negotiations, Versailles, with the advent of the German delegates, more than ever riveted the gaze of an expectant world. To sign or not to sign, or, in the words of Wilhelm Shakespeare, *Sein oder nicht sein: hier ist die Frage*—that was the problem which from the moment of his famous opening speech Count Brockdorff-Rantzau was up against. But, as the days wore on, in spite of official impenitence and the double breach of the Armistice terms by the scuttling of the German war-ships at Scapa and the burning of the French flags at Berlin, the force of "fierce reluctant truculent delay" was spent against the steadily growing volume of national acquiescence, culminating in the decision of the Weimar Assembly, the tardy choice of new delegates, and the final scene in the Hall of Mirrors, haunted by the ghosts of 1871.

Writing at the moment of the Signature of Peace and in deep thankfulness for the relief it brings to a stricken world, Mr. Punch is too old to jazz for joy, but he is young enough to face the future with a reasoned optimism, born of a belief in his race and their heroic achievements in these great and terrible years. Victory took us by surprise; and we were less prepared for Peace at that moment than we had ever been for War. And just as in the first days of the fighting we went astray, running after the cry "Business as usual," so to-day we are making as bad a mistake when we run after "Pleasure as usual"—or rather more than usual. But we soon revised that early error, and we shall not waste much time about revising this. For though we lacked imagination then, and still lack it, we have the gift, perhaps even more useful if less showy, of commonsense. And when commonsense is found in natures that are honest and hearts that are clean, it may make mistakes, but not for long. No, the spirit which won the War is not going to fail us at this second call. Perhaps we have only been waiting for the actual coming of Peace to settle down to our new and greater task.

But let us never forget the debt, unpaid and unpayable, to our immortal dead and to the valiant survivors of the great conflict, to whom we owe freedom and security and the possibility of a better and cleaner world.

ALSO AVAILABLE FROM NONSUCH PUBLISHING

Alexander, Boyd (ed.)	*The Journal of William Beckford in Portugal and Spain*	978 1 84588 010 1
Brontë, Rev. Patrick	*The Letters of the Rev. Patrick Brontë*	978 1 84588 066 8
Broughton, S.D.	*Letters from Portugal, Spain and France*	978 1 84588 030 9
Brunel, Isambard	*The Life of Isambard Kingdom Brunel, Civil Engineer*	978 1 84588 031 6
Coleman, E.C. (ed.)	*The Travels of Sir John Mandeville, 1322–1356*	978 184588 075 0
Corbett, Sir Julian	*The Campaign of Trafalgar*	978 1 84588 059 0
Duff, Charles	*A Handbook on Hanging*	978 1 84588 141 2
Eyre, Lt Vincent	*The Military Operations at Cabul*	978 1 84588 012 5
Fothergill, A. Brian	*Beckford of Fonthill*	978 1 84588 085 9
Fothergill, A. Brian	*Sir William Hamilton: Envoy Extraordinary*	978 1 84588 042 2
Gooch, Sir Daniel	*The Diaries of Sir Daniel Gooch*	978 1 84588 016 3
Greenwood, Lt John	*The Campaign in Afghanistan*	978 1 84588 004 0
Hammond, J.L. and Barbara	*The Village Labourer*	978 1 84588 056 9
Hawkes, Francis L.	*Commodore Perry and the Opening of Japan*	978 1 84588 026 2
Helps, Sir Arthur	*The Life and Labours of Thomas Brassey*	978 1 84588 011 8
Hill, Wg Cdr Roderic	*The Baghdad Air Mail*	978 1 84588 009 5
Hudson, W.H.	*Idle Days in Patagonia*	978 1 84588 024 8
Jefferies, Richard	*Wildlife in a Southern County*	978 1 84588 064 4
Livingstone, David and Charles	*Expedition to the Zambesi and its Tributaries*	978 1 84588 065 1
Matthews, Henry	*Diary of an Invalid*	978 1 84588 017 0
Park, Mungo	*Travels in the Interior of Africa*	978 1 84588 068 2
Scott, Capt. Robert F.	*The Voyage of the Discovery, Vol. One*	978 1 84588 057 6
Ségur, Gen. Count Philippe de	*Memoirs of an Aide de Camp of Napoleon, 1800–1812*	978 1 84588 005 7
Simmonds, P.L.	*Sir John Franklin and the Arctic Regions*	978 1 84588 007 1

For forthcoming titles and sales information see

www.nonsuch-publishing.com